ARCO

TYPING and KEYBOARDING for EVERYONE

Nathan Levine

Sheryl Lindsell-Roberts, Editor

MACMILLAN • USA

TO THE BEGINNER

Typing and Keyboarding for Everyone will teach you to type by touch—without looking at your fingers. These lessons "work." They were tested for ten years on 3,000 beginners, ages 14 to 70: students, clerks, cashiers, bookkeepers, salespeople, nurses, technical assistants, and workers in all sorts of jobs and occupations. All of them learned how to type quickly and expertly.

Type a lesson a day. Learn a few keys at a time; then as you practice words, sentences, and paragraphs, your control of those keys becomes automatic. Before you know it, you are a touch typist.

Here are some of the special features you will like about this book:

1. **Entirely Self-Teaching:**
   Each lesson is short, simple, and easy to master; it tells you plainly what to do and how to do it; it is your own private home tutor.

2. **Cumulative Review:**
   Beginning with Lesson 2, you review all the keys you have learned; you reinforce your control of those keys before you go on to the new ones. You can see your day-to-day progress toward your goal of typing mastery.

3. **Accuracy and Speed-Building in Same Lesson:**
   You get intensive accuracy and speed-building practice in the same lesson to develop your maximum typing skill. Interesting, flowing copy helps you reach specific goals.

4. **Word-Counted Material:**
   Sentences, paragraphs, and 1- to 5-minute copy tests tell you at a glance how many words you have typed in a given time.

5. **Timed-Typing Score Sheet:**
   A simple, easy-to-use score sheet for 1-, 2-, 3-, 4-, and 5-minute timed tests lets you see your day-to-day progress in speed-with-accuracy.

6. **Realistic Business Letter Placement:**
   No complicated scales to memorize. An all-purpose letter-placement formula tells you how to arrange quickly and attractively ALL styles of business letters.

7. **Typing Aids:**
   Basic office "Know-Hows"—to help you become a proficient typist.

8. **Computer Savvy:**
   Exercises & hints for using your computer.

Eleventh Edition

An Arco Book

Copyright © 1998, 1996, 1994, 1992, 1989, 1985, 1980, 1978, 1976, 1974, 1971 by Nathan Levine

ARCO is a registered trademark of Simon & Schuster, Inc.
MACMILLAN is a registered trademark of Macmillan, Inc.

Manufactured in the United States of America

1 2 3 4 5 6 7 8 9 10

Library of Congress Number: 97-81013

ISBN: 0-02-862194-8

Macmillan Reference USA
A Simon & Schuster Macmillan Company
1633 Broadway
New York, NY 10019-6785

CONTENTS

PROGRESS CHART FOR TIMINGS

DATE	PAGE	WPM	ERRORS	DATE	PAGE	WPM	ERRORS

INTRODUCTION

In the 1950's, computers took up entire rooms and were about as personal as warehouses. Even Thomas Watson, former Chairman of IBM, once said, "I think there is a world market for maybe five computers." How wrong was he?

As we enter the new millennium, PCs are practically necessities. Computers serve as a link to people all over the world. Companies are requiring them, neighbors are buying them, and children are lagging behind without them.

So, pack up your typewriter, ship it off to the Smithsonian, and join the computer generation. That's exactly what we've done with this book. (The former editions aren't being shipped off to the Smithsonian, but we've joined the computer generation and have removed all references to typewriters.)

Not only has technology changed, but attitudes have changed. Typing was once reserved for secretaries. Today, everyone from students to CEOs must know how to type. Learn to type as if your career depends on it; it just might.

Sheryl Lindsell-Roberts, Editor

HARDWARE AND SOFTWARE

Hardware

Get to know your computer and refer to its user's manual for any questions. There are many features at your fingertips that you didn't have on a typewriter. A major change will be your output, or hard copy.

In the olden days of typewriters, your keystrokes would appear directly on paper. If you made a typo, you'd erase the original, shield and erase the copies, struggle to squeeze or expand what you needed to change, and have a finished copy that was less than perfect. Or, you'd have to start over again.

On a computer, your keystrokes appear on the screen. You can change to your heart's content, move paragraphs and pages, and press "print" when you're comfortable with the text. No one will be any the wiser for what you originally typed.

Software

There are probably more features in your software than you'll ever use. You'll be able to cut, copy, or paste words and paragraphs; prepare tables of contents and indexes automatically; generate charts and tables; insert graphics; and much more. Here are just a few features you might enjoy:

Different font styles

Try *italic*, **bold**, ***bold italic***, ALL CAPS, SMALL CAPS, serif, sans serif, ^{superscript}, $_{subscript}$, or ~~strikethrough~~ (for drafts).

12. **Final F and FE**
    To Form the Plural:

    A. Add *s:* roof-roofs; chief-chiefs; giraffe-giraffes
        OR:

    B. Change the *f* to *v* and add *s* or *es:*
        life-lives; knife-knives; thief-thieves

13. **Final CE or SE?**
    When the noun and verb are similar:

    A. Write *ce* in nouns: advice, device, prophecy

    B. Write *se* in verbs: advise, devise, prophesy

14. **QU Combination**
    Always write *u* after *q:* acquit, banquet, question

15. **US or OUS?**

    A. Write *us* in nouns: callus, fungus, phosphorus

    B. Write *ous* in adjectives: callous, serious, tedious

16. **ABLE or IBLE?**

    A. Write *able* if you can form a word ending in *ation:* durable-duration; irritable-irritation

    B. Write *ible* if you can form a word ending in *ion, tion,* or *ive:* accessible-accession; collectible-collection; digestible-digestive

17. **CEED, CEDE, or SEDE?**
    CEED is only in: exceed, proceed, succeed
    SEDE is only in: supersede
    CEDE is in all other words: concede, intercede, precede,
    recede, secede

18. **Plural of Nouns**

    A. In most nouns, form the plural by adding s:
        house-houses; teacher-teachers

    B. In nouns ending in s, sh, ch, and x, add es:
        bus-busses; brush-brushes; watch-watches; box-boxes

19. **Plural of Compound Nouns**

    A. If the noun consists of one word, add s: cupful-cupfuls
        spoonful-spoonfuls

    B. If the noun consists of more than one word, add s to the principal word:

        mother-in-law   editor-in-chief
        mothers-in-law   editors-in-chief

20. **Prefixes and Suffixes Ending in ll**
    Omit one *l* in joining to other words: all-altogether
    full-wonderful

Shading

You might want to accent a portion of your text with shading. You can go from very light to very dark. This is 5%.

Borders

You can put borders around text. Select different line thicknesses or a shadow box, which you see here.

Automatic Bullets

- Dots
- Arrows
- Filled diamonds
- Outlined diamonds
- Stars

Symbols

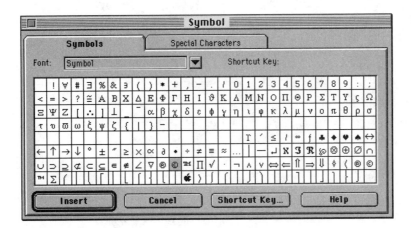

NOTE: In this book, we'll be showing screen shots from Microsoft Word. Most word processing software packages have similar functions. Refer to your user's manual for specific instructions on the function being discussed.

B.   Drop the final *e* before a suffix beginning with a vowel:
     admire-admirable; desire-desirable; please-pleasure

EXCEPTIONS: notice-noticeable; change-changeable
              dye-dyeing; singe-singeing

5. **Final C**
   Add *k* before joining to *ed, er, ing,* or *y:*
      picnic-picnicked-picnicker-picnicking
      panic-panicky

6. **Final CE**
   Keep the *e* before *able:*   peace-peaceable
                                    service-serviceable

7. **Final GE**
   Keep the *e* before *ous:*   courage-courageous
                                    outrage-outrageous

8. **Final OE**
   Keep the *e* before a suffix beginning with any vowel except *e:*
      hoe-hoeing-hoed
      toe-toeing-toed

9. **Final N**
   Keep the *n* before *ness:*   mean-meanness
                                    sudden-suddenness

10. **Final O**
    To Form the Plural:

    A.   If the *o* is after a vowel, add *s:*   cameo-cameos
                                                    radio-radios

    B.   If the *o* is after a consonant, add *s* or *es:*
                                                    piano-pianos
                                                    tomato-tomatoes

11. **Final Y**
    To Form the Plural:

    A.   If the *y* is after a vowel, add *s:*   railway-railways
                                                    attorney-attorneys

    B.   If the *y* is after a consonant, change *y* to *i* and add *es:*
         vacancy-vacancies
         country-countries

    NOTE: Keep the *y* before *ing:*   testify-testifying
                                            accompany-accompanying

Computer Keyboard

The Backspace, Enter, and Shift keys are enlarged for convenience and located in their familiar Selectric positions.

Dedicated function control keys are provided for frequently used functions such as Print Screen, Scroll Lock, and Pause.

The Escape key is isolated at the upper left of the keyboard to help reduce keying errors.

The dedicated Numeric Pad includes its own Enter key and four Arithmetic Function keys, making it simple to work with numbers only.

The Tab and Caps Lock keys are enlarged and are located in their familiar Selectric positions.

Function keys are located across the top of the keyboard and spaced in groups of four. Two additional Function keys provide added flexibility in host access or communication applications.

Two Ctrl and Alt keys—one on each side of the space bar—offer easy access with either hand.

Screen Control and Cursor keys are separated from the numeric pad for easier, faster access.

GENERAL SPELLING RULES

The following rules, without all the exceptions, provide a general guide to correct spelling and are adequate in most cases. When in doubt, use a good dictionary.

1. **Adding Prefixes and Suffixes**

   A. A prefix is one or more letters added to the beginning of a word to change its meaning:

   il + legal = illegal   un + noticed = unnoticed
   im + mortal = immortal   dis + approve = disapprove

   B. A suffix is one or more letters added to the end of a word to change its meaning:

   sing + er = singer   pay + able = payable
   usual + ly = usually   heat + ing = heating

   C. Words may be divided at the end of a line on the prefix: de-duct, pre-paid, re-lease; or on the root: fly-ing, near-est, room-mate. A root is a word from which others are derived. Fly is the root of flying; near is the root of nearest; room is the root of room-mate.

2. **Doubling Final Consonants**

   A. In words of one syllable ending in a vowel and a consonant (except *h* or *x*), double the final consonant before *ed, er, est, ing*:

   plan   planned   planner   planning
   hot   hotter   hottest

   B. In words of more than one syllable ending in a vowel and a consonant and accented on the last syllable, follow the same rule as for words of one syllable: Double the final consonant before *ed, er, est, ing*:

   control   controlled   controller   controlling   controllable
   regret   regretted   regretting   regrettable

3. **EI or IE?**

   A. Write *ei* after *c* when the sound is *ee:*   deceit, deceive, ceiling, conceive, perceive, receive, receipt

   B. Write *ie* after other letters: belief, believe, chief, fiend, grief, mischief, pierce, relieve, reprieve, shriek, sieve

   Exceptions: counterfeit, feign, foreign, forfeit, freight, height, heinous, leisure, neighbor, neither, reign, seize, sleigh, their, veil, vein, weight, weird

4. **Final E**

   A. Keep the final e before a suffix beginning with a consonant:
   hope-hopeful; care-careless; manage-management

   Exceptions: awe-awful; due-duly; whole-wholly; judge-judgment; argue-argument; acknowledge-acknowledgment

COMPUTER TERMINOLOGY

Alphanumeric	A combination of alphabetic and numeric characters.
Batch	A collection of similar work that can be produced in a single operation.
Bit	The smallest unit of information.
Buffer	The device in the computer that compensates for the rate of data flow.
Byte	A sequence of bits, usually shorter than a word.
CD	Compact disc that holds large amounts of information.
Character	A letter, number, symbol, or space.
Command	Instructions to the equipment to perform a certain function.
CPS	Characters per second (speed of typing).
CPU	Central processing unit (memory in a computer).
Crash	To become inoperable.
CRT	Cathode ray tube (a television-like screen for the display of characters).
Cursor	The movable indicator on a CRT that indicates the place for editing a document.
Cyberspace	The metaphoric space where electronic communications take place.
Database or Data Base	Files of information used by an organization.
Debug	To locate and remove errors.
Delete	To remove a character, word, line, etc.
Disk (Diskette)	Equipment for the computer that is used for the recording, transcribing, and storage of data.
Down Time	Period of time during which equipment is inoperable.
Edit	To revise text.
E-mail	(Electronic mail) Electronic messages from one person or group to another.
FAX	The transmission and receipt of text and or graphics through telephone lines.
Field	A group of characters related for a specific purpose, somewhat like a column.
Floppy Disk	A disk used to store and retrieve programs and data.
Font	An assortment of characters in a certain type and size.
Hard Copy	Paper copy.
Hardware	The equipment.
Input	Information that is entered into a system; to enter information into a system.
Interface	The connection of two or more systems or devices.
I/O	Input/Output.
Internet	A network of computers that relay information, allowing users to send and receive transfer files worldwide.

5. Numbers ten and lower
   used as street names:

   Martin lives at 490 Tenth Avenue.

6. Numbers used as proper
   names:

   David is in the Twelfth Regiment.

7. Indefinite sums of money:

   Al needs several hundred dollars.

8. Fractions standing alone:

   Mark ran three-fourths of a mile.

9. Numbers 10 and lower,
   except when used with
   numbers above 10:

   We need 25 books on English; 9 on
   Mathematics; 7 on Economics; 8 on
   French; 4 on Drawing; 3 on Latin.
   I will need at least four copies.

10. Time of day used informally:
    Time of day used with o'clock:

    I saw Jim at a quarter past four.
    Meet me at seven o'clock tonight.

Keyboarding	Typing on a computer.
Menu	A selection of tasks.
Modem	Hardware that connects the computer to telephone lines for sending and receiving information.
Net	Shortened version of the Internet.
Output	The final results that are produced.
Software	Programs and routines needed to give instructions to the hardware.
Store	Place in memory or on disk.
Terminal	A device that can send and receive information.
URL	(Uniform Resource Locator) The address of an Internet site.
WWW	(World Wide Web) The part of the Net with multimedia capabilities.

Personal Computer (PC)

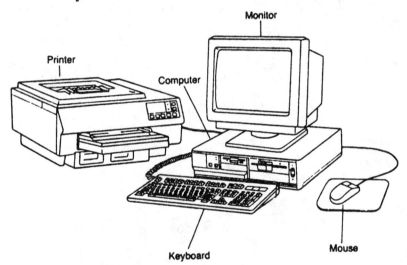

Keyboard	The placement of alphabetic and numeric keys is standard and conforms to any typewriter keyboard. Many keyboards have an additional ten-key numeric pad (similar to a calculator) for faster numeric entry.
Computer	The "brains" of the unit that receives commands from the keyboard. It serves as the central location for the storage and processing of data.
Monitor	The monitor, also known as a CRT, display screen, or VDT, is a television-like screen for the display of text.
Mouse	A hand-held device, connected to the computer, that controls images on the display screen. It can be used to replace the keyboard for many functions.
Printer	The printer, which gives you paper copy.

RULES FOR TYPING NUMBERS

Type in Figures:

1. All sums of money—round numbers without ciphers:

   Max borrowed $2,175 to buy a car.
   Her ballpoint pen costs 98 cents.

2. Percentages and decimals:

   The highest rate was 4.8 percent.

3. Numbers after nouns:

   Act 4; Scene 2; Track 6; Room 12.

4. House numbers, except house number One:

   Paul moved to 325 Stanton Street.
   Walt moved to One Delaney Street.

5. Measures, weights, distances, degrees, dimensions:

   10 quarts; 125 pounds; 650 miles.
   The temperature is 8° Fahrenheit.
   Our living room is 14 by 25 feet.

6. Numbers above ten:

   We ordered 11 more Spanish books.

7. Order, Invoice, Policy, Serial numbers—all without commas:

   Order No. 1623; Invoice No. 4958;
   Policy No. 5670; Serial No. 2079.

8. Numbers above ten used as street names. Endings **th, nd, st,** should be omitted:

   Ben lives at 50 West 11 Street.
   Ralph lives at 39-68 52 Avenue.
   Josephine lives at 472 91 Road.

9. Numbers and fractions in a series:

   Ship 5 bags, 10 boxes, 15 crates.
   1/2, 2/3, 3/4, 1/9, 2 5/6, 10 3/5

10. Time used with a.m. and p.m.*:

    We plan to arrive home at 10 p.m.

11. The larger of two numbers used together:

    Robert needs 50 five-cent stamps.

12. Exact age in years, months, days:

    15 years 10 months 17 days old.

13. Graduation and historical dates:

    The class of '57. Spirit of '76.

14. Decades and centuries:

    The gay 1890's. The 9th century.

*May also be used as AM and PM without periods.

Type in Words:

1. A number that begins a sentence:

   Seventy boys entered the contest.

2. Round numbers, except when used in advertising:

   About one hundred men were there.
   Our sale offers you 100 bargains.

3. Approximate ages:

   Dr. Hartley is about thirty-five.

4. Isolated numbers ten and lower:

   Sidney lived ten years in Berlin.

GET READY TO KEYBOARD

1. Clear your workstation of everything you do not need.

2. Prop your typing book in an upright position.

3. Sit all the way back on your chair. Your back should be straight.

4. Place your feet flat on the floor.

5. Place your elbows close to your body. Your forearms should be parallel to the keyboard.

6. Your wrists should be low, just clearing the keyboard.

7. Your body should be centered opposite the J-key.

8. Hold your head erect, facing your book.

9. *Left Hand*
   Place your fingertips on the **A S D F** keys. Draw the left thumb close to the first finger.

10. *Right Hand*
    Place your fingertips on the **J K L ;** keys. Extend your right thumb above the center of the space bar.

    Hint: In order to avoid stress to your body, it is important to move around every 15–20 minutes.

12. **Business Letters**

A. Address: Capitalize all titles in the address.

```
Mr. Harry Nevins, Manager
```

B. Salutation: Capitalize the first and last words, titles, and proper names in the salutation.

```
Dear Sir
Ladies and Gentlemen
Dear Mr. Davis
```

C. Complimentary Close: Capitalize only the first word in the complimentary close.

```
Sincerely yours,
Yours very truly,
```

D. Closing Lines: Capitalize the title if it follows the name of the writer.

```
Thomas Ashton          Thomas Ashton, President
President
```

LESSON 1
HOME KEYS
A S D F   J K L ;
Left hand   Right hand

| A | S | D | F | | | J | K | L | : ; |

Throughout this book, leave the 1.25" default margins for right and left margins. Refer to your user's manual for instructions on how to change margins.

HOW TO STRIKE THE KEYS

Tap each key lightly and quickly using a flat-oval motion. Hold your fingers slightly above (not on) the keys. The keys respond instantly to very light strokes. If you hold a key down too long, it will repeat.

Follow each numbered step exactly.

1. **F-Key Tryout:** *Use Left First Finger.*
   Type the following **f**'s:

   ffffffffff

2. **J-Key Tryout:** *Use Right First Finger.*
   Type the following **j**'s:

   jjjjjjjjjj

3. **Space Bar Tryout:** *Use Side of Right Thumb.*
   To leave a space after a letter or a word, strike the space bar sharply with the side of your right thumb.

   Type the following **f j** alternately. Space sharply after each letter. Bounce the thumb off the space bar.

   ffffffffffjjjjjjjjjj f j f j f j f j f j f j f j

6. **Historical Documents, Events, Monuments**
Capitalize historical documents, events, and monuments:

```
Declaration of Independence
Battle of Gettysburg
Statue of Liberty
```

7. **Seasons of the Year**
Do not capitalize: spring . . . summer . . . autumn . . . winter

8. **Geographical Names and Names of Buildings**
Capitalize geographical names and names of buildings:

```
East River
Atlantic Ocean
Rocky Mountains
Empire State Building
```

Do not capitalize east, west, north, or south when used to indicate direction:

```
Drive north on Broadway, then turn west on 42 Street.
```

9. **Companies, Organizations, Institutions, Government Agencies**
Capitalize the names of companies, organizations, institutions, and government agencies:

```
Arco Publishing
American Automobile Association
Columbia University
Federal Communications Commission
```

10. **Nouns**

   A. Capitalize a noun when it is part of a specific name:
      ```
      Bentley School
      ```

   B. Capitalize all proper nouns and their derivatives:
      ```
      Mexico................ Mexican
      South................. Southerner
      Elizabeth............ Elizabethan
      ```

11. **Languages, Religions, The Deity**
Capitalize languages, religions, and words denoting the Deity:

```
Spanish
Mohammedan
God
```

4. **Enter Practice:**

A. Swiftly extend the little finger of your right hand to the enter key.

B. Lightly tap the enter key, making the cursor move down to the next line.

C. Move the finger back home.

Type the following line 5 times.

Try to do the A B C steps in one quick 1-2-3 motion.

```
fff jjj fff jjj fff jjj fff jjj fff jjj fff jjj fj
```

5. **Home-Key Practice:** Type the following lines exactly. Double space after each 2-line group by using the return key twice. Doing so will leave one blank line between groups.

```
FIRST       fff jjj fff jjj fff jjj fff jjj fff jjj fff jjj fj    Return to
FINGER:     fff jjj fff jjj fff jjj fff jjj fff jjj fff jjj fj    the margin
                                                                  without
                                                                  spacing at
SECOND      ddd kkk ddd kkk ddd kkk ddd kkk ddd kkk ddd kkk dk    end of a
FINGER:     ddd kkk ddd kkk ddd kkk ddd kkk ddd kkk ddd kkk dk    line.


THIRD       sss lll sss lll sss lll sss lll sss lll sss lll sl
FINGER:     sss lll sss lll sss lll sss lll sss lll sss lll sl


FOURTH      aaa ;;; aaa ;;; aaa ;;; aaa ;;; aaa ;;; aaa ;;; a;
FINGER:     aaa ;;; aaa ;;; aaa ;;; aaa ;;; aaa ;;; aaa ;;; a;
```

NOTE: On a computer you will have a wordwrap feature. This means that if text is too long to fit on a line, the next complete word will automatically return (wrap) to the left margin of the next line.

RULES FOR CAPITALIZATION

1. **General Rule**

   A. Capitalize the first word of a complete sentence:

   ```
   Mr. Hale is our office manager.
   ```

   B. Capitalize the first word of a quoted sentence:

   ```
   He said, "Mr. Hale is our office manager."
   ```

   NOTE: Do not capitalize the first word of a quotation if it is not a complete sentence:

   ```
       He said that Mr. Hale is "our office manager."
   ```

   Do not capitalize the first word of a quotation that is resumed within a sentence:

   ```
   "I'll phone Joe," she said, "while you dress."
   ```

2. **After a Colon**
   Capitalize the first word after a colon if that word begins a complete sentence:

   ```
   Here is Mr. Hale's message: Mail all the letters today.
   ```

3. **Titles of Persons**

   A. Capitalize a title when it applies to a specific person:

   ```
   President Clinton signed the welfare bill.
   ```

   B. Capitalize a title standing alone if it is of high distinction:

   ```
   The President vetoed the welfare bill.
   The Governor will speak to us tonight.
   ```

4. **Titles of Publications**
   (Books, Magazines, Newspapers, Articles, Plays, etc.)
   Capitalize the first word and every important word in the title:

   ```
   Sixty Years on the Firing Line (book)
   Death of a Salesman (play)
   ```

5. **Dates, Months, Holidays**
   Capitalize the days of the week, months of the year, and holidays:

   ```
   Friday
   December
   Christmas
   ```

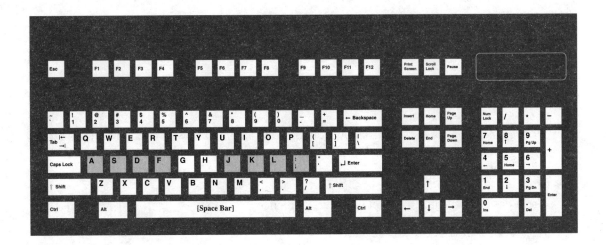

6. **Test Your Skill:** Type the following lines exactly. Double space after each 2-line group by using the enter key twice.

```
fff aaa ddd fad fad fad; jjj aaa lll jal jal jal;
fff aaa ddd fad fad fad; jjj aaa lll jal jal jal;
```
Space once after a semicolon.

```
aaa lll aaa lll all all; ddd aaa ddd dad dad dad;
aaa lll aaa lll all all; ddd aaa ddd dad dad dad;
```

```
sss aaa ddd sad sad sad; aaa sss kkk ask ask ask;
sss aaa ddd sad sad sad; aaa sss kkk ask ask ask;
```

```
a fad; ask dad; ask a lad; jal asks; a lad falls;
a fad; ask dad; ask a lad; jal asks; a lad falls;
```
All the home keys.

```
all fads; alda asks; a sad lass; jal asks a lass;
all fads; alda asks; a sad lass; jal asks a lass;
```

10. Use a hyphen in a series of hyphenated words having the same ending:

```
We get first-, second-, and third-class mail.
```

The Dash

NOTE: Most software programs allow you to create an em dash with either a symbols menu or a keyboard command. If yours does not, just type two hyphens. There should be no space before or after a dash.

1. Use a dash to indicate an abrupt break in a sentence:

```
Mr. Pearson left--where did he go?
```

2. Use a dash for emphasis:

```
Kelly--the youngest child--is quite spoiled.
```

3. Use a dash to set off a short, final summary:

```
She had only one pleasure--dancing.
```

4. Use a dash to indicate the name of an author after a direct quotation:

```
"To sin by silence when they should protest makes cowards out of
men."--Abraham Lincoln
```

5. Use a dash to set off an explanatory group of words:

```
His food--nuts, berries, fish--kept him alive.
```

LESSON 2
E U

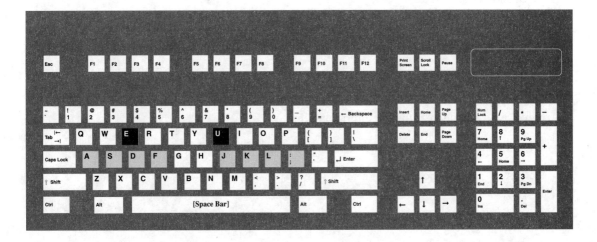

1. **Review**: Type each line twice. Double space after each 2-line group.

```
fff jjj ddd kkk sss lll aaa ;;; fdsa jkl; fdsajkl;
fad fad jal jal sad sad lad lad dad dad asks asks;
add add; dad dad; fall fall; asks asks; lass lass;
ask ada; ask jal; dad asks a lad; a sad lad falls;
ask a lad; jal asks a sad lad; a sad lad asks dad;
```

Always keep eyes on copy. Think of the finger and the key it controls.

2. **New-Key Practice**: **E** *Use D-Finger.*
   Practice the reach from **D** to **E** and back home to **D.** Keep the **A**-finger on its home key. When you can reach **E** without looking at your fingers, type each line twice:

Double space after each 2-line group.

```
e e e e ded ded ded ded; fed fed fed; led led led;
ded ded ded elk elk elk; jed jed jed; elf elf elf;
ded ded ded fee fee fee; see see see; ale ale ale;
ded ded ded lea lea lea; sea sea sea; eke eke eke;
fed led elk jed elf fee; see ale lea; sea jed eel;
```

Space once after a semicolon.

3. **New-Key Practice: U** *Use J-Finger.*
   Practice the reach from **J** to **U** and back home to **J.** Keep the **L** and **;** fingers on their home keys. When you can reach **U** without looking at your fingers, type each line twice:

```
u u u u juj juj juj juj; dud dud dud; due due due;
juj juj juj uke uke uke; use use use; sue sue sue;
juj juj juj jud jud jud; ula ula ula; auk auk auk;
juj juj juj flu flu flu; due due due; sud sud sud;
use dud due sud jud flu; eke auk ula; sue due use;
```

Return fingers quickly to home keys.

Exclamation Point

1. Use an exclamation point to express strong feeling or emotion:

   ```
   Welcome home, son!
   Rush, it's urgent!
   ```

The Hyphen

1. Use a hyphen to divide a word at the end of a line. Make the division between syllables. Never type a hyphen at the beginning of a line.

2. Use a hyphen to join words serving as a single adjective *before* a noun:

   ```
   He is a well-known writer.
   ```

3. Use a hyphen in spelling fractions serving as modifiers:

   ```
   The job is two-thirds done.
   ```

   ```
   But:  Two thirds of the job is done.
   ```

4. Use a hyphen in spelling the compound numbers twenty-one through ninety-nine.

5. Use a hyphen to form compound verbs:

   ```
   Double-check every entry.
   Do not side-step your duty.
   ```

6. Use a hyphen with **ex** and **elect:**

   ```
   ex-President Johnson
   Mayor-elect Smith
   ```

7. Use a hyphen to avoid a confusing union of letters:

   ```
   re-enter
   pro-ally
   ```

8. Use a hyphen in compound nouns consisting of three or more words:

   ```
   brother-in-law
   teacher-in-charge
   ```

9. Use a hyphen in compound words beginning with **self:**

   ```
   a self-explanatory letter
   a self-addressed envelope
   ```

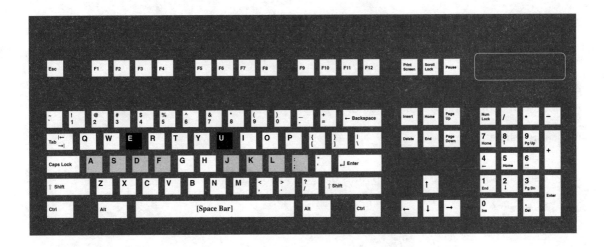

4. **Boost Your Skill:**

   A. Type each line 3 times.

   B. Practice words that have errors.

   C. Try for a PERFECT copy of both lines.

All the keys you know.

```
ask sue; a full fee; use a desk; see a jade flask;
feed jal a salad; sue sells flasks; ella asks sue;
```

Keyboard at a steady, even pace.

3. Use an apostrophe to indicate feet and minutes after figures:

```
Hy made the mile in 5'.
The block is 125' long.
```

4. Use an apostrophe to indicate the omission of numbers:

```
the spirit of '76
```

5. Use an apostrophe to indicate plurals of figures and letters:

```
5's
A's
```

Parentheses

1. Use parentheses to enclose explanatory or added information:

```
In our office (and in most offices) the full block style business
letter is used.
```

2. Use parentheses to enclose enumerated items:

```
Employers seek workers who are (1) accurate, (2) dependable, and
(3) productive.
```

3. Use parentheses to enclose figures after amounts that are spelled out:

```
The monthly rent is two hundred dollars ($200).
```

Question Mark

1. Use a question mark after a direct question:

```
Do you know his address?
```

But: After a question which is in the form of a request, use a period.
```
May we have your check next week.
Will you please mail an estimate.
```

2. Use a question mark with parentheses to express doubt or uncertainty concerning a statement immediately preceding:

```
He was born May 10, 1892 (?).
```

LESSON 3
R I

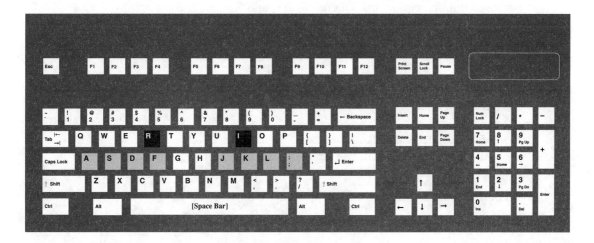

1. **Review:** Type each line twice. Double space after each 2-line group.

```
fff jjj ddd kkk sss lll aaa ;;; ded juj ded juj eu
ale elk jud use jake dues fuel fuse fake sulk jade
ask sue; a full fee; use a desk; see a jade flask;
a lad sees; a lad sees a duel; jud sells us seeds;
see us; sue sees us; use a desk; use a full flask;
```

Space quickly.

Keep elbows close to body.

2. **New-Key Practice: R** *Use F-Finger.*

Remember: Double space after each 2-line group.

Practice the reach from **F** to **R** and back home to **F.** Keep the **A S D** fingers in home position. When you can reach **R** without looking at your fingers, type each line twice.

```
r r r r frf frf frf frf; fur fur fur; jar jar jar;
frf frf frf are are are; ark ark ark; red red red;
frf frf frf rue rue rue; ear ear ear; ref ref ref;
frf frf frf era era era; ere ere ere; far far far;
red ark fur rue jar ref ear raj era are ruse lurk;
```

Type the first copy of each line slowly; then a little faster on the second.

3. **New-Key Practice: I** *Use K-Finger.*

Practice the reach from **K** to **I** and back home to **K.** Keep semicolon-finger in home position. When you can reach **I** without looking at your fingers, type each line twice.

```
i i i i kik kik kik kik; irk irk irk; sir sir sir;
kik kik kik kid kid kid; air air air; fir fir fir;
kik kik kik rid rid rid; ail ail ail; lid lid lid;
kik kik kik die die die; aid aid aid; lie lie lie;
air fir kid sir rid rue lid lie aid ail sail jail;
```

Return to the margin without looking up.

The Apostrophe

1. Use an apostrophe to show possession:

   (a) In singular and plural nouns not ending in *s,* add *'s:*
   ```
   boy's shoes
   men's coats
   ```

   (b) In singular nouns ending in *s,* add an apostrophe only:
   ```
   Dickens' novels
   Charles' papers
   OR add 's: Dickens's novels
               Charles's papers
   ```
   The first form seems preferred. Both are correct.

   (c) In plural nouns ending in *s,* add an apostrophe only:
   ```
   lawyers' offices
   ```

   NOTE: In plural company and organization names that are possessive, omit the apostrophe:
   ```
   Teachers College
   Bankers Trust Co.
   ```

   (d) In compound words, add *'s:*
   ```
   father-in-law's car
   ```

   (e) In joint ownership, add *'s* to the last name only:
   ```
   Sue and Laura's room
   ```

   (f) In separate ownership, add *'s* to each name:
   ```
   Sue's and Laura's rooms
   ```

   (g) In indefinite pronouns, add *'s:*
   ```
   one's best efforts
   each other's rights
   ```

   NOTE: Do not use an apostrophe with possessive personal pronouns:
   ```
   his, hers, its, ours, yours, theirs
   ```

2. Use an apostrophe to indicate a contraction:
   ```
   isn't (is not)
   wasn't (was not)
   ```

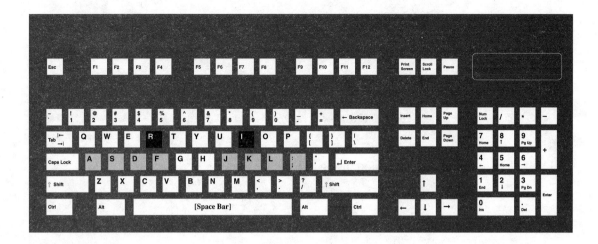

4. **Boost Your Skill:**

   A. Type each line 3 times.

   B. Practice words that have errors.

   C. Try for a PERFECT copy of both lines.

```
all is fair; sell us jars; a kid used a real idea;   All the keys
fill a jar; fill a red jar; fill all red jars full   you know.
```

2. Use quotation marks to enclose direct quotations:

    Emerson said, "The only way to have a friend is to be one."

3. Use quotation marks to enclose each separate speech:

    "I am sure," he said, "that we have met before."

    RULE: Put the comma and period inside quotation marks.

4. Use quotation marks to enclose special words—for emphasis:

    I will check "debit"; you will check "credit."
    Our company's "slogan": QUALITY FIRST--ALWAYS

    RULE: Put the semicolon and colon outside quotation marks.

5. Use an apostrophe to enclose a quotation within a quotation:

    Thomas said, "The command 'Don't give up the ship' was given by
    John Paul Jones."

6. In a long quotation, use quotation marks only at the beginning of each paragraph and at the end of the last paragraph.

7. WITH QUESTION MARK

    A. If the entire sentence is a question, put the question mark outside the quotation marks:
        Did Harry say, "I have just mailed the letter"?

    B. If only the quotation is a question, put the question mark inside the quotation marks:
        Mr. Farley inquired, "Has the manager arrived?"

8. WITH EXCLAMATION MARK

    A. If the entire sentence is an exclamation, put the exclamation mark outside the quotation marks:
        How foolish it is for the neighbors to "argue"!

    B. If only the quotation is an exclamation, put the exclamation mark inside the quotation marks:
        Ken Riley shouted, "Dave hit another home run!"

LESSON 4
G O

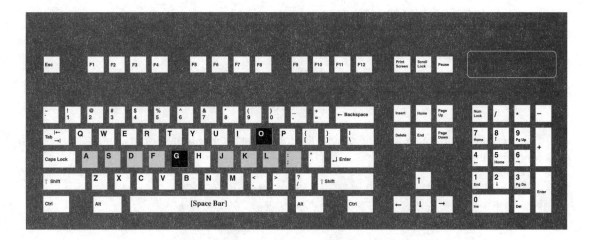

1. **Review:** Type each line twice. Double space after each 2-line group.

```
frf juj ded kik sss lll aaa ;;; frf juj ded kik ri      Hit space bar.
sir rue lid due ail jar kid ire fur auk jerk raid;
all is fair; sell us jars; a kid used a real idea;
russ is ill; fred uses skill; jed said alf is safe
all kids; all kids like; all kids sure like sleds;
```

2. **New-Key Practice: G** *Use F-Finger.*
   Practice the reach from **F** to **G** and back home to **F.** Keep the **A S D** fingers in home position.
   When you can reach **G** without looking at your fingers, type each line twice:

```
g g g g fgf fgf fgf fgf; jug jug jug; rug rug rug;      Move fingers back to
fgf fgf fgf dig dig dig; leg leg leg; fig fig fig;      home keys.
fgf fgf fgf sag sag sag; dug dug dug; gag gag gag;
rig rig rig egg egg egg; jig jig jig; keg keg keg;
jug jig rug fig age lug jag gas keg rag flag glad;
```

3. **New-Key Practice: O** *Use L-Finger.*
   Practice the reach from **L** to **O** and back home to **L.** Keep the **J**-finger in home position.
   When you can reach **O** without looking at your fingers, type each line twice:

```
o o o o lol lol lol lol; old old old; oaf oaf oaf;
lol lol lol dog dog dog; oak oak oak; oar oar oar;
lol lol lol sol sol sol; jog jog jog; roe roe roe;
log log log joe joe joe; oil oil oil; our our our;
oil old dog jog sol log doe roe oaf foe golf goal;
```

4. Use a semicolon before such introductory expressions as **for example, namely, such as:**

   ```
   You need to do much research before you can write the speech; for
   example, you must read some books on the subject.
   ```

5. Use a semicolon to connect two short related sentences:

   ```
   Let's camp here; there's a lake nearby.
   ```

The Colon

1. Use a colon to introduce a listing when "the following" is mentioned or implied—except following the verb:

   ```
   I bought these items: a tie, a shirt, and a hat.
   My favorite subjects are typing, gym, and English.
   ```

2. Use a colon to introduce a question:

   ```
   What I wish to know is: Are you a touch typist?
   ```

   NOTE: Capitalize the first word after the colon if it is part of a complete sentence.

3. Use a colon to separate hours and minutes in expressing time:

   ```
   We arrived home at 2:30 a.m.
   ```

4. Use a colon after such expressions as **namely, for example, as follows,** if a series or a statement follows:

   ```
   We shall place our order with you on one condition, namely: The
   entire lot must be shipped within ten days after receipt of the
   order.
   ```

5. Use a colon after the salutation in business letters for mixed punctuation:

   ```
   Dear Sir:
   Dear Mr. Smith:
   Ladies and Gentlemen:
   ```

Quotation Marks

1. Use quotation marks to enclose titles of articles, plays, poems, essays, lectures, and the like:

   ```
   I have read the article "Campus Revolution."
   ```

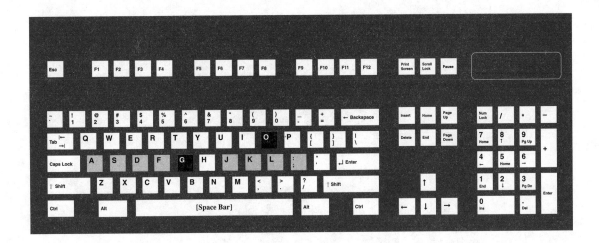

4. **Boost Your Skill:**

    A. Type each line 3 times.

    B. Practice words that have errors.

    C. Try for a PERFECT copy of both lines.

```
gail uses jugs; gail uses old jugs for salad oils;    All the keys you
joe seeks four dark jade rugs for four glad girls;    know.
```

6. Use a comma to indicate the omission of a word:

```
Henry is tall; Walter, short.
```

7. Use a comma to separate two words or figures that may be confusing:

```
To Robert, Thomas was a perfect gentleman.
In 1941, 30 ships were lost in one day.
Instead of 25, 52 men applied for the job.
```

8. Use a comma to separate thousands, millions, billions—except in order numbers, invoice numbers, serial numbers, policy numbers:

```
3,791    25,132    4,392,690    2,365,930,038
```

9. Use a comma between title and name of organization if **of** or **of the** has been omitted:

```
President, New York University
Superintendent, Board of Education
```

10. Use a comma before conjunctions such as **and, but, for, or, neither,** and **nor** when they join two independent clauses:

```
Many are called, but few are chosen.
Ted shaved quickly, for he was late.
```

The Semicolon

1. Use a semicolon between independent clauses not joined by a conjunction:

```
We may not go after all; we may stay home.
```

2. Use a semicolon between clauses joined by parenthetical expressions such as **therefore, however, otherwise, nevertheless** if the expression could start a new sentence:

```
Mr. Roe is very well-known here; nevertheless, we cannot extend
unlimited credit to him.
```

NOTE: Use a comma after the parenthetical expression.

3. Use a semicolon to separate a series of phrases or clauses that contain one or more commas:

```
The boys enjoyed their vacation in many ways; in the morning, by
fishing; in the afternoon, by playing tennis; and in the evening,
by indoor games.
```

LESSON 5
Shift Keys . (Period)

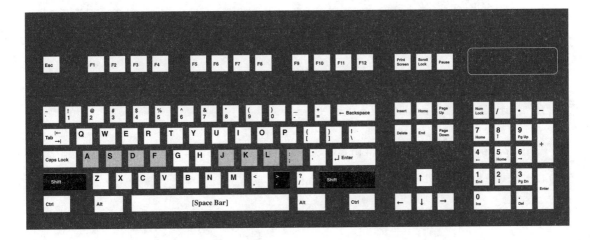

1. **Review:** Type each line twice. Double space after each 2-line group.

All the keys you know.

```
fdsa jkl; fdsa jkl; ask lad jal fad sad fall flask
frf juj ded kik fgf lol rig due old jugs kegs rode
all is fair; sell us jars; a kid used a real idea;
gail uses jugs; gail uses old jugs for salad oils;
joe seeks four dark jade rugs for four glad girls;
```

Keep your wrists as motionless as possible. Let your fingers do the work.

2. **New-Key Practice: Left Shift Key** *Use A-Finger.*
   To capitalize a letter typed by your right hand:

   (1) Stretch **A**-finger to shift key, keeping **F**-finger at home.

   (2) Hold shift key down while you type letter to be capitalized.

   (3) Release shift key—move fingers to home keys.

   Type each line twice:

   ```
   J J Ja Ja Jal Jal Jal; K K Ki Ki Kid Kid Kid;
   L L Lo Lo Lou Lou Lou; U U Ul Ul Ula Ula Ula;
   I I Id Id Ida Ida Ida; O O Ol Ol Ole Ole Ole;
   ```

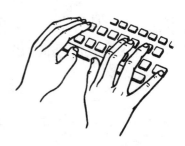

Hold shift key down until you have struck and released the key for the capital letter.

3. **New-Key Practice: Right Shift Key** *Use ;-Finger.*
   To capitalize a letter typed by your left hand:

   (1) Stretch **;**-finger to shift key, keeping **J**-finger at home.

   (2) Hold shift key down while you type letter to be capitalized.

   (3) Release shift key—move fingers to home keys.

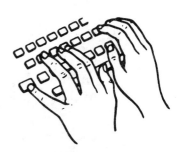

RULES FOR PUNCTUATION

The Period

1. Use a period after a statement:

   The material will be shipped today.

2. Use a period after an abbreviation:

   Mr. Bradley is moving to St. Louis.

3. Use a period for a decimal point in numbers:

   Our overtime rate is $6.50 an hour.

4. Use a period after each initial in a person's name, spacing only once:

   Mr. E. S. Goldman will call on you.

The Comma

1. Use a comma to separate words, phrases, or clauses in a series:

   The display consists of rings, watches, and bracelets.

2. Use a comma after an introductory word, phrase, or clause:

   However, I am inclined to agree with you.
   In the meantime, we have decided to wait.
   After I endorsed the check, he mailed it.

3. Use a comma to set off a word, phrase, or clause that is not essential to the thought in a sentence:

   Our manager, Mr. Ralph Dix, is on vacation.
   Her mother, who is in Paris, telephoned me.

4. Use a comma to set off words in direct address:

   Will you, Mr. Hampton, write the letter?

5. Use a comma before short direct quotations:

   He said, "I am leaving for London tomorrow."

Type each line twice:

```
F F Fa Fa Fae Fae Fae; G G Gu Gu Gus Gus Gus;
D D De De Del Del Del; S S Sa Sa Sal Sal Sal;
A A Al Al Alf Alf Alf; R R Ro Ro Rod Rod Rod;
```

Depress shift key firmly.

4. **New-Key Practice: . (Period)** *Use L-Finger.*

Space once after the period.

Practice the reach from **L** to Period and back home to **L**. Curl the **L**-finger as it goes downward. Keep the **J**-finger in home position. When you can reach the period without looking at your fingers, type each line twice:

```
. . . . 1.1 1.1 1.1 1.1 Jr. Jr. Jr. Sr. Sr. Sr.
Dr. Dr. Dr. Ed. Ed. Ed. Fr. Fr. Fr. Rd. Rd. Rd.
```

Jr. for Junior
Sr. for Senior
Dr. for Doctor
Ed. for Editor or Education
Fr. for French
Rd. for Road

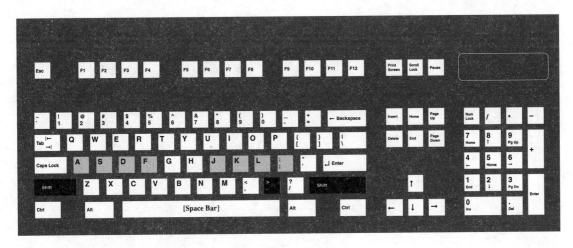

5. **Boost Your Skill:**

   A. Type each line twice—smoothly.

   B. Practice words that have errors.

   C. Start over. See how many perfect pairs of lines you can turn out.

All the keys you know.

```
Joel fed us. See Dr. Gold. Lou asked for a salad.
Gus seeks oil. Gus seeks a jug of oil for Gloria.
Lou sold all four dogs. Jo said dogs fear a gale.
Ed uses a desk file. A desk file is good for all.
All skills are good. All skills are good if used.
```

Space once after a period at the end of a sentence.

Lesson 5: Shift Keys . (Period)

10. Use the spell checker. It won't catch everything but it will catch a lot.

11. Try reading from bottom to top or from right to left; working in reverse often helps you to spot typos.

12. Re-read the document after you've gotten some distance from working on it.

> EXAMPLE: Re-read it the following day if time allows. If not, take a five- or ten-minute break, then re-read it.

LESSON 6
T H

1. **Review:** Type each line twice. Double space after each 2-line group.

```
fdsa jkl; fdsa jkl; ask sad lad jal fad fall flask
frf juj ded kik fgf lol rig due old jugs kegs rode
Flo Gus Del Sue Alf Rod Ella Joe Kid Lou Ole Ulaf;
Joe fed us. See Dr. Gold. Lou asked for a salad.
All skills are good. All skills are good if used.
```

All the keys you know.

Return to the margin without looking up.

2. **New-Key Practice: T** *Use F-Finger.*
   Practice the reach from **F** to **T** and back home to **F.** Keep the **A** and **S** fingers in home position. When you can reach **T** without looking at your fingers, type each line twice:

```
t t t t ftf ftf ftf ftf; fit fit fit; lot lot lot;
ftf ftf ftf rut rut rut; jet jet jet; kit kit kit;
ftf ftf ftf tea tea tea; sit sit sit; tug tug tug;
toe toe toe dot dot dot; ate ate ate; jut jut jut;
fit lot rut jet kit tea sit tug dot jut true tire;
```

Eyes on copy. Be a touch typist.

3. **New-Key Practice: H** *Use J-Finger.*
   Practice the reach from **J** to **H** and back home to **J.** Keep the **K L ;** fingers in home position. When you can reach **H** without looking at your fingers, type each line twice:

```
h h h h jhj jhj jhj jhj; hut hut hut; her her her;
jhj jhj jhj hat hat hat; had had had; she she she;
jhj jhj jhj hag hag hag; hoe hoe hoe; ash ash ash;
hue hue hue hit hit hit; hot hot hot; the the the;
hug hoe has hat hid she rush josh fish hook hills;
```

12 Tips for Careful Proofreading

Your ability to proofread is critical. One typographical error (known as a *typo*) or one improperly placed punctuation mark can completely change the meaning of your message.

> *Typo (w instead of t)*
>
> I will now go to the meeting.
>
> I will not go to the meeting.
>
> *Improperly placed colon*
>
> Execution: impossible to be pardoned
>
> Execution impossible: to be pardoned

The following are hints for proofreading thoroughly and accurately.

1. Scan the document with an eye for format and style.

   EXAMPLE: If you used the full block letter style, is everything left justified?

2. Check the spelling of people's names, including middle initials and titles.

   EXAMPLE: Did you write *Mr.* instead of *Ms.* or spell *Glenn* with two n's instead of one?

3. Pay special attention to numbers.

   EXAMPLE: Did you tell the reader he/she owes you $7,115.00 instead of $7,515.00?

4. Keep an eye out for misused or misspelled homonyms.

   EXAMPLE: Did you use *their* instead of *there?*

5. Look for repeated words.

   EXAMPLE: Perhaps you wrote, "I will call Mr. Jones in in a week."

6. Be on the alert for small words that are misspelled. We tend to read what we know should be there.

   EXAMPLE: It's easy to type *at* instead of *as* and not notice the error.

7. Check dates.

   EXAMPLE: If you wrote Monday, July 10, be certain July 10 is a Monday.

8. Check for omissions.

   EXAMPLE: Did you leave off an area code, zip code, or other critical piece of information?

9. If you're proofreading a technical or statistical document, it's best to use the buddy system. If no one is available to help, read the document with a ruler (line by line) checking it against the source of the information.

4. **Boost Your Skill:**

    A. Type each line 3 times.

    B. Practice words that have errors.

    C. Try for a PERFECT copy of both lines.

```
Joel got to that lake at four. He hooked a trout.
Ask Gil or Kurt to look for Hale at the old house.
```

5. **Figure Your Speed:** You can tell how fast you type by timing yourself, or by having someone time you.

    A. Note the word-count scale below. It shows that every 5 characters—letters, numbers, punctuation marks, and spaces—count as 1 average word. The scale shows that each of the 2 lines above it has 10 words.

    B. If you type the first line in 1 minute, your speed is 10 words a minute. If you type both lines in 1 minute, your speed is $2 \times 10 = 20$ words a minute.

    C. If you type part of a line, note the number below where you stopped; it tells you how many words to count for that part of the line.

    EXAMPLE: Let's say that in the 1-minute timing below, you typed the first line and had to stop after typing the word "right" in the second line. Your speed would be:

10 words in line 1

<u>6</u> words in line 2

16 words in 1 minute

6. **Test Your Skill:** Take Three 1-Minute Timings.

Follow these steps in all your 1-minute timings.

    A. Repeat if you finish before end of 1 minute.

    B. After each timing, jot down total words typed and total errors. Count only 1 error in a word even if it has more.

    C. Practice the words that have errors till they are easy for you.

    D. Record on your Progress Chart for Timings (page 136) your best speed within 3 errors.

    GOAL: 15 words a minute within 3 errors.   WORDS

All the keys you know.

```
Jill has a silk skirt. Her sister got it for her.    10
The skirt fits her just right. Dora likes it too.    20
      1     2     3     4     5     6     7     8     9     10
```

M E M O R A N D A̶C̶ ᵁᴹ

To: All Personaᵉˡ ~~le~~ *mel*

From: Marc A. Laurence

Date: September 30,

    Subject: Office Supplies [*margin*

It has come to my attention that many office supplies ~~has~~
have been missing lately. Now that many of your ~~kids~~ are ∧ *children*
back in school for the fall term, the condition has
worsened.

Unfortunately, you have left me no choice but to enforce the
following policy: No one is allowed in the supply room without my secretary, Miss Sullivan, accompanying them. ~~Me and~~
She and I ~~her~~ are the only ones who will have keys to the supply
room.

We deeply regret having to take this action, but we are
certain that you will see why it is necessary.

sll

M E M O R A N D U M

To: All Personnel

From: Marc A. Laurence

Date: September 30, _____

Subject: Office Supplies

It has come to my attention that many office supplies have
been missing lately. Now that many of your children are back
in school for the fall term, the condition has worsened.

Unfortunately, you have left me no choice but to enforce the
following policy: No one is allowed in the supply room without my secretary, Miss Sullivan, accompanying them. She and I
are the only ones who will have keys to the supply room.

We deeply regret having to take this action, but we are certain that you will see why it is necessary.

sll

LESSON 7
W Y , (Comma)

1. **Review:** Type each line twice. Double space after each 2-line group.

```
fgf jhj fdsa jkl; fgf jhj fdsa jkl; fgf jhj fg jh;
frf juj ftf jhj fgf kik ded lol ss aa l. l. l. l.l
jug led for ask sag hit jet out sol tug goes salt;
Jill has a silk skirt. Her sister got it for her.
The skirt fits her just right. Dora likes it too.
```

Return fingers quickly to home keys. Keep elbows close to body.

2. **New-Key Practice: W** *Use S-Finger.*
    Practice the reach from **S** to **W** and back home to **S.** Keep the **F**-finger close to its home key. Try to hold elbow close to body. When you can reach **W** without looking at your fingers, type each line twice:

```
w w w w sws sws sws sws; sow sow sow; low low low;
sws sws sws was was was; few few few; row row row;
sws sws sws wag wag wag; how how how; jaw jaw jaw;
who who who wit wit wit; dew dew dew; awl awl awl;
dew row was law few wag how jaw wit wed work slow;
```

Type at a steady, even pace.

3. **New-Key Practice: Y** *Use J-Finger.*
    Practice the reach from **J** to **Y** and back home to **J.** Keep the **K L ;** fingers in home position. When you can reach **Y** without looking at your fingers, type each line twice:

```
y y y y jyj jyj jyj jyj; yet yet yet; yak yak yak;
jyj jyj jyj shy shy shy; sly sly sly; way way way;
jyj jyj jyj try try try; why why why; dry dry dry;
yes yes yes jay jay jay; sly sly sly; fry fry fry;
guy say dye you key lay joy toy hay day eye yield;
```

Use finger-reach action only; arms and hands still.

The following memorandum contains many errors in both content and form. Use the proofreader's marks on page 111 to indicate the necessary changes. Then, type the memorandum correctly. (The corrections and the corrected memorandum appear on page 117).

```
                    M E M O R A N D A


To: All Personal

From: Marc A. Laurence

Date: September 30, ____

     Subject: Office Supplies

     It has come to my attension that many office supplies has
     have been missing latley. Now that many of your kids are
     back in school for the Fall term, the condition has
     worstened.

     Unfortunately you have left me no choise but to enforse the
     following policy: Noone is allowed in the supply room with
     out my secretary, Miss sullivan, accompanying them. Me and
     her are the only one's who will have keys to the supply
     room.

     We deeply regret having to take this action but we are
     certain that you will see why it is necessary.

     sll
```

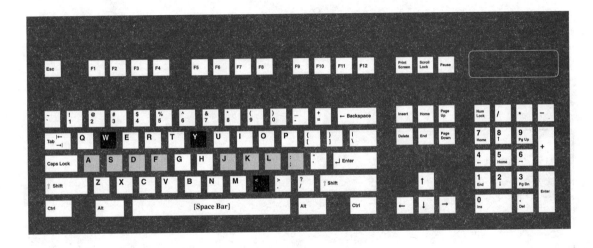

4. **New-Key Practice: , (Comma)** *Use K-Finger.*
   Practice the reach from **K** to **,** and back home to **K.** Curl the **K**-finger as it goes downward. Keep the **;**-finger in home position. When you can reach the **,** without looking at your fingers, type each line twice:

All the keys you know.

```
, , , k,k k,k k,k yak, yak, yak; lark, lark, lark;
k,k k,k k,k work, work, work; sheik, sheik, sheik;
jerk, fork, dark, silk, lurk, stork, freak, Greek;
```

Space once after a comma and semicolon.

5. **Boost Your Skill:**

   A. Type each line smoothly 3 times.
   B. Practice words that have errors.
   C. Try for a PERFECT copy of both lines.

```
Yes, Walt took the test. He told Jud it was easy.
Take the ferry, Edward. You will get there early.
```

All the keys you know.

6. **Test Your Skill:** Take Three 1-Minute Timings.

   GOAL: 15 words a minute within 3 errors.
   Record your best speed within 3 errors.

WORDS

All the keys you know.

```
Try to do the work just right if you do it at all.    10
Good daily work is a sure way to get to your goal.    20
         1   2   3   4   5   6   7   8   9   10
```

12 Seventh Avenue
Ridgefield Park, NJ 07660
June 16, _____

Mrs. Janice Teisch
Business Manager
Real World Counseling Service
134 Fourth Avenue
New York, NY 07081

Dear Mrs. Teisch:

Your sales manager, Betty Feiler, has informed me that your company will soon be adding to its secretarial staff. Please consider me a candidate for one of the positions.

Your company could no doubt benefit from a person experienced in dealing with the public and trained in shorthand and typing--in addition to having a bookkeeping background.

Although my enclosed resume supports my claims, I know there will be questions it cannot answer. May I request an interview at your earliest convenience.

Sincerely yours,

Lynne Sullivan

Enclosure

LESSON 8
Q P : (Colon)

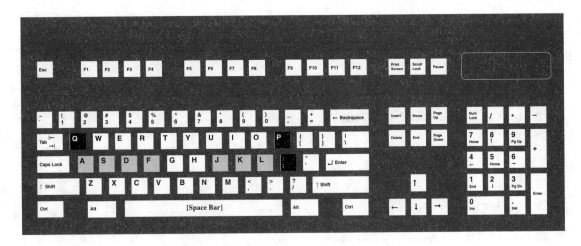

1. **Review:** Type each line twice. Double space after each 2-line group.

```
frf juj ftf jyj fgf jhj ded kik sws lol aaa ;;; wy    Type smoothly—
kit yet lid why fir how use sir tow jig lye aid so    without pausing.
The daily drills will aid you to get to your goal.
Yes, Flora; Judith does her task with great skill.
Walter told Jerry Hale that he hooked a huge fish.
```

2. **New-Key Practice: Q** *Use A-Finger.*
Practice the reach from **A** to **Q** and back home to **A.** Keep the **F**-finger on its home key. Keep elbow close to your side. When you can reach **Q** without looking at your fingers, type each line twice:

```
q q q q aqa aqa aqa aqa; aqua aqua; quotes quotes;    Sit straight. Keep
aqa aqa aqa quit quit; quail quail; liquor liquor;    wrists low without
aqa aqa aqa quay quay; quite quite; quaffs quaffs;    touching keyboard.
aqa aqa aqa quid quid; quirk quirk; quires quires;
quit quid quad quest quote quite quilt quash quake
```

3. **New-Key Practice: P** *Use ;-Finger.*
Practice the reach from **;** to **P** and back home to **;**. Keep the **J K** fingers close to their home keys. Keep elbow close to your side. When you can reach **P** without looking at your fingers, type each line twice:

```
p p p p ;p; ;p; ;p; ;p; pal pal pal; pit pit pits;    Keep right thumb
;p; ;p; ;p; pay pay pay; par par par; pie pie pie;    curved, close to the
;p; ;p; ;p; put put put; pig pig pig; paw paw paw;    space bar.
pep pep pep sip sip sip; hip hip hip; fop fop fop;
lip fop sap hip gyp dip put kip paw rip jeep quip;
```

12 7th Avenue   *Seventh*
Ridgefield Park, NJ   07660 [*2 Spaces*
June 16,

Mrs. Janice Teisch
Business manager
Real World Counseling Service
134 Fourth Avenue
New York, NY 07081
Dear ~~Miss~~ Teisch   *Mrs.*

Your sales manager, Bunny Feiler, has informed me that your ~~your~~
company will soon be adding to its secretarial staff. Please
consider me a candidate for one of the position*s*

Your company (no doubt could) benefit from a person experienced in
dealing with the public and trained in shorthand and typing--in
~~edition~~ to having a bookkeeping background.
addition

Although my enclosed resume supports my claims, I know ~~their~~ will   *there*
be questions it cannot answer. May I request an interview at
your earliest convenience.

                    Sincerly yours,   *e*

                                    [*at*

                                    Margin

            Lynne Sullivan

Enclosure

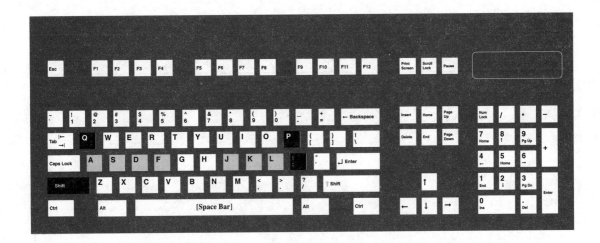

4. **New-Key Practice: : (Colon)** *Use ;-Finger.*
   To type the colon, depress the left shift key and strike the ;-key.

EXAMPLES: Foods we like: grapes, eggs, soda.   Space once after a
           We also like: yogurt, fish, pears.   colon.

Type each line twice:

: : : ;:; ;:; ;:; Dear Gay: Dear Pal: Dear Kurt: All the keys you
Dear Joe: Walt stayed at Hotel Quill till Friday. know.

5. **Boost Your Skill:**

   A. Type each line 3 times—smoothly.
   B. Practice words that have errors.
   C. Try for a PERFECT copy of both lines.

Judge Paul K. Quale did free the slow, tired jury.   Space once after a
Joe Yale will take Paula Quat to the party Friday.   period following a
                                                     capital initial.

6. **Test Your Skill:** Take Three 1-Minute Timings.

GOAL: 15 words a minute within 3 errors.
       Record your best speed within 3 errors.   WORDS

All the keys   Dear Joe: Gus Quill says he types all the letters   10
you know.   for his father. This work surely tests his skill.   20
                  1   2   3   4   5   6   7   8   9   10

The following letter contains many errors in both content and form. Use the proofreader's marks on page 111 to indicate the necessary changes. Then, type the letter correctly. (The corrections appear on page 114, and the final letter is on page 115.)

---

12 7th Avenue
Ridgefield Park, NJ 07660
June 16, _____

Mrs. Janice Teisch
Business manager
Real World Counseling Service
134 Fourth Avenue
New York, NY 07081

Dear Miss Teisch,

Your sales manager, Betty Feiler, has informed me that your your company will soon be adding to its secretarial staff. Please consider me a candidate for one of the position.

Your company no doubt could benifit from a person expereinced in dealing with the public and trained in shorthand and typing-- in edition to having a bookeeping background.

Although my enclosed resume supports my claims, I know their will be questions it can not answer. May I request an interview at your earliest convenience.

Sincerly yours,

Lynne Sullivan

NOTE: Don't forget to run your program's spelling checker.

LESSON 9
C V / (Slant)

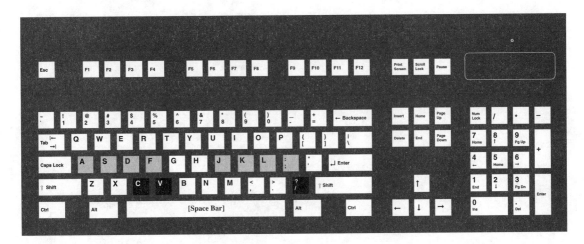

1. **Review:** Type each line twice. Double space after each 2-line group.

```
frf juj ftf jyj fgf jhj ded kik sws lol aqa ;p; qp
word fish joke quay girl harp quit glad tops equal
Look at your work; it tells you how well you type.
We will offer all help to the quiet lad who works.
Judge Kurt P. Quays will free the slow jury today.
```

All the keys you know.

Space quickly after each word.

2. **New-Key Practice: C** *Use D-Finger.*
   Practice the reach from **D** to **C** and back home to **D**. Curl the **D**-finger as it reaches down to **C**. Keep the **A**-finger in home position. When you can reach **C** without looking at your fingers, type each line twice:

```
c c c c dcd dcd dcd dcd; cut cut cut; cue cue cue;
dcd dcd dcd cur cur cur; cud cud cud; cup cup cup;
dcd dcd dcd cat cat cat; cap cap cap; cow cow cow;
dcd dcd dcd cod cod cod; ice ice ice; cog cog cog;
cut cap cog cry cod cow cash jack calf tack quick;
```

In the word *ice,* line 4, move D-finger from C to E without pausing on home key.

3. **New-Key Practice: V** *Use F-Finger.*
   Practice the reach from **F** to **V** and back home to **F**. Keep the **A S D** fingers in home position. When you can reach **V** without looking at your fingers, type each line twice:

```
v v v v fvf fvf fvf fvf; via via via; vow vow vow;
fvf fvf fvf vet vet vet; vie vie vie; eve eve eve;
fvf fvf fvf Vic Vic Vic; Val Val Val; vat vat vat;
pave pave pave; void void void; Vicki Vicki Vicki;
rave vows jive gave have five caves quiver voyage;
```

After the corrections have been made, the copy on page 111 will read as follows:

If you are planning to go to work in an office after graduation from high school, take all the business subjects offered. Typing, shorthand, English, business arithmetic, and bookkeeping are essential for most office jobs. They help a *beginner* get a good start in the business world. Try to EXCEL in them.

Test your aptitude for office work while you are in school. Take part in its administrative, clerical, and bookkeeping functions. Also, try to get an office job during vacations. Whatever business experience you can get will give you a good chance to find out first hand what office work is like.

So prepare now by taking advantage of your high school years to build a firm foundation for SUCCESS.

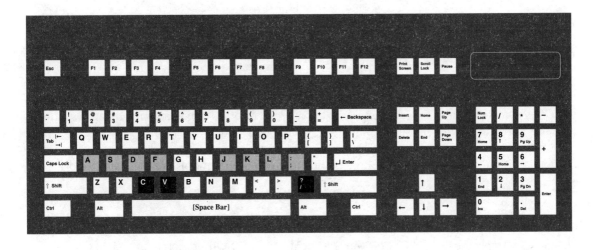

4. **New-Key Practice: / (Slant)** *Use ;-Finger.*

Practice the reach from **;** to **/** and back home to **;**. Keep the **J**- and **K**-fingers in home position. When you can reach the **/**-key without looking at your fingers, type each line twice:

```
/ / / / ;/; ;/; ;/; c/o c/o; c/l c/l; s/s s/s s/s     c/o = care of
;/; ;/; ;/; his/yours his/yours; we/they we/they;     c/l = car lots
                                                       s/s = steamship
```

5. **Paragraph Practice:** Double Spacing.

A. Type each paragraph slowly, smoothly.

B. Practice each word that has an error.

C. Try for a PERFECT copy of each paragraph.

WORDS

Set line spacing at "double."
```
    Skill grows at a quiet pace. Hurry is waste.        10
Type at such a rate that you feel at perfect ease.      20
     1    2    3    4    5    6    7    8    9    10
```

WORDS

```
    Type at a very steady pace, without pauses or       10
jerks. This is how you will develop a good skill.       20
     1    2    3    4    5    6    7    8    9    10
```

6. **Test Your Skill:** Take Three 1-Minute Timings.

GOAL: 15 words a minute within 3 errors.
       Record your best speed within 3 errors.

Single-Spaced, Blocked Paragraph.
Set line spacing at "single."

LESSON 33
PROOFREADER'S MARKS

You may sometimes have to type a revised copy of typed or printed matter. Some notations indicating the corrections will be self-explanatory; others will consist of special symbols known as proofreader's marks. These symbols are often used by writers, editors, and businesspeople. Each correction is indicated in the copy. Some of the more common symbols are illustrated below.

¶	Paragraph	#	Leave a space	∧	Insert
≋	Capital letter(s)	⌐	Move to left	⊙	Insert period
∿ or ᴛ𝓻	Transpose	⌐	Move to right	⌃	Insert comma
ᵧ	Take it out	𝓁𝒸	Small letter	⌃	Insert semicolon
stet	Don't change	⊔	Lower this letter	?	Insert question mark
◠	Close up	⊓	Raise this letter	!	Insert exclamation mark

Placing Proofreader's Marks

¶ If you are planning to go ~~directly~~ to work in an office

after graduation from high school, take all the business

subjects offered. typing, shorthand, English, Business

arithmetic and bookkeeping are essential for most office

jobs. They help a beginner get a good start in the busi-

ness world. Try to ~~excel~~ *excel* in ~~those subjects~~ *them*.

Test your aptitude for office work while you are in

school. Take part in its ~~administrative~~ *stet*, clerical, and

⌐bookkeeping functions. Also, try to get an office job

⌐during vacations. Whatever business experience you can get

will give you a good ch ance to find out first hand ⌐hat

office work is like⊙

#
So prepare now by taking advantage of your high
∧

school years to build a firm foundation for success.

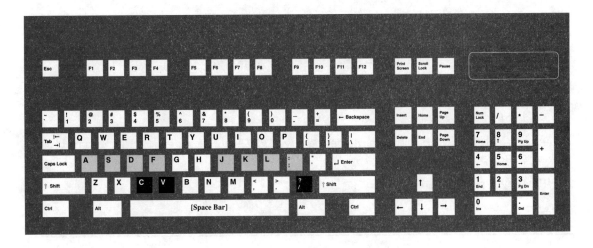

All the keys
you know.

Dear Vicki: Pat Garvy takes the speed test today.   10
Jud Quat is out of practice; he will try it later.   20

       1   2   3   4   5   6   7   8   9   10

NOTE: Use the "tab" key to indent. Refer to your user's manual for instructions on setting tabs.

WORKS CITED

[1]Hawley, Ellis. *The Great War and the Search for a Modern Order.*
   (New York: St. Martin's Press, 1979), p. 3.

[2]Snowman, Daniel. *America Since 1920.* (New York: Harper & Row,
   1968), p. 23.

[3]Hicks, John. *Republican Ascendancy 1921–1933.* (New York: Harper
   & Row, 1960), p. 85.

[4]Hawley, p. 26.

WORKS CONSULTED

Harwick, Arthur, *War and Social Change in the Twentieth Century,*
   New York: St. Martin's Press, 1974.

Hawley, Ellis, *The Great War and the Search for a Modern Order,*
   New York: St. Martin's Press, 1979.

Hicks, John, *Republican Ascendancy 1921–1933,* New York: Harper &
   Row, 1960.

Murphy, Paul L., *World War I and the Origin of Civil Liberties in
   the United States,* New York: W. W. Norton & Company, 1923,
   1979.

Snowman, Daniel. *America Since 1920,* New York: Harper & Row,
   1968.

LESSON 10
B M X

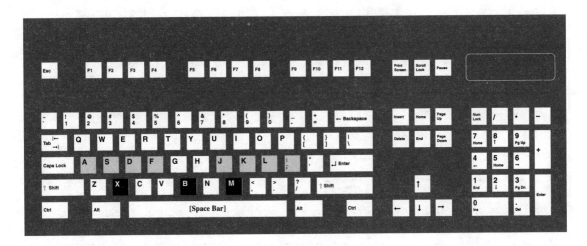

Line 3:
Move
D-finger
from C to E
and F-finger
from R to V
without
pausing on
home key.

1. **Review:** Type each line twice. Double space after each 2-line group.

```
fr ju ft jy fg jh de ki sw lo aq ;p fv ;/ fv dc ;/
fist jerk cave hogs quit wade yule aqua kegs pelt;
vice vice vice slice slice slice curve curve curve
If you wish to keep a secret, keep it to yourself.
Every day is a good day if you put it to good use.
```

Try to type each
repeat line a little
faster.

2. **New-Key Practice: B** *Use F-Finger.*
Practice the reach from **F** to **B** and back home to **F.** Keep the **A S D** fingers in home position.
When you can reach **B** without looking at your fingers, type each line twice:

```
b b b b fbf fbf fbf fbf; but but but; bid bid bid;
fbf fbf fbf bag bag bag; boy boy boy; bow bow bow;
fbf fbf fbf bar bar bar; bus bus bus; cub cub cub;
lab lab; bug bug bug; fob fob fob; quibble quibble
hub web big buy pub rib jab rub tub ebb bake above
```

Hit space
bar.

3. **New-Key Practice: M** *Use J-Finger.*
Practice the reach from **J** to **M** and back home to **J.** Keep the **K L ;** fingers in home position.
When you can reach **M** without looking at your fingers, type each line twice:

```
m m m m jmj jmj jmj jmj; mad mad mad; may may may;
jmj jmj jmj mug mug mug; mop mop mop; Mac Mac Mac;
jmj jmj jmj vim vim vim; hum hum hum; mal mal mal;
aim aim aim met met met; mow mow mow; rim rim rim;
gym mob mud gum jam sum him mar milk qualm flames;
```

Move J-finger from U
to M; from M to U
without pausing on
home key.

METAMORPHOSIS WORLD WAR I

    If one studies history, one is at some point confronted with the question of what factors cause times of calm and those of rapid change. It is an irony of history that periods of great progress have often come immediately following war. Many wars have brought changes, but no war brought as much change as did World War I (WWI). WWI most changed the previously isolated United States. Through economic, social, and political change resulting from WWI, the United States developed into a world power.

INDUSTRIAL REVOLUTION

    During the American Industrial Revolution, the economy grew tremendously. Industrial production per person rose three times, and national industrial production rocketed to eight times what it was in 1870.[1] England still remained the world's leading economic power, despite America's fantastic gains. When WWI broke out, the allies soon became dependent on American goods. American industries were called upon to be the "arsenal of democracy." Because of this demand, America emerged from the war as the world's leading economic power.[2]

    One of the important results of the war was the gains made by the workers and trade unions. Before the war, unions had been looked upon as a source of local trouble that was to be dealt with by local authorities.

    During the war, unions were successful in gaining higher wages through collective bargaining and arbitration--instead of through crippling strikes. This contributed to greater union membership and greater respect for unions. After the war there were occasions when strikes became necessary. The strike became a more powerful weapon because both industry and the public had become dependent upon unions. Thus, if a union threatened to strike, much greater consideration was paid to the union's demands than had been before the war.[3]

    At the onset of the war, when industry was called upon to shift production into high gear, the response was confusion and disorder. The government was compelled to take temporary wartime control of some vital industries to insure maximum efficiency. While in control, the government instituted some good work policies that were carried over to peacetime and have survived right up to today. Some of these were as follows: an eight-hour work day, time and a half for overtime, less employee discontent, and expanded employee welfare benefits.[4]

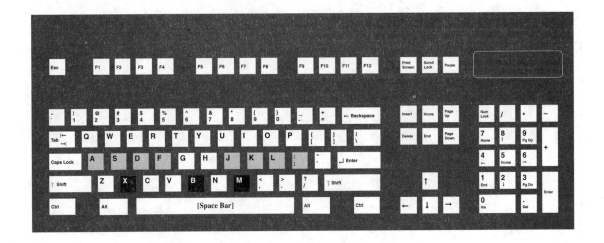

4. **New-Key Practice: X** *Use S-Finger.*
Practice the reach from **S** to **X** and back home to **S.** Curl the **S**-finger as it reaches to **X.** Keep the **F**-finger in home position. When you can reach **X** without looking at your fingers, type each line twice:

```
x x x x sxs sxs sxs sxs; six six six; tax tax tax;     Hold hands parallel
sxs sxs sxs box box box; lax lax lax; wax wax wax;     to the slant of the
pox pox pox vex vex vex; hex hex hex; axe axe axe;     keyboard.
fox fox fox Dix Dix Dix; Cox Cox Cox; Rex Rex Rex;
sex mix axe wax pox lax fox hex box flux Max Xmas;
```

5. **Paragraph Practice:**
Try for a PERFECT copy of each paragraph.   WORDS

```
    Aim to excel. Do your daily task to the best       10
of your ability. Good work leads to a happy life.      20
Remember: Success comes if you strive quite hard.      30
      1    2    3    4    5    6    7    8    9   10
```

```
    To develop a skill takes time, of course. So      10
devote as much time as possible to your daily work     20
here. Have faith. Expert skill will come to you.       30
      1    2    3    4    5    6    7    8    9   10
```

6. **Test Your Skill:** Take Three 1-Minute Timings.

GOAL: 15 words a minute within 3 errors.
Record your best speed within 3 errors.

Single-Spaced, Blocked Paragraph.
Set line spacing at "single."   WORDS

All the keys   ```
you know.   Dear Paul: Jack said he will meet you at the ball   10
               game Friday. Vic Quay will take you home by taxi.   20
                 1   2   3   4   5   6   7   8   9   10
               ```

**Lesson 10: B M X**                                        23
               ```

SAMPLE MANUSCRIPT

METAMORPHOSIS--WORLD WAR I

Marc A. Lindsell
Social Studies

March 25, ____

LESSON 11
Z N ?

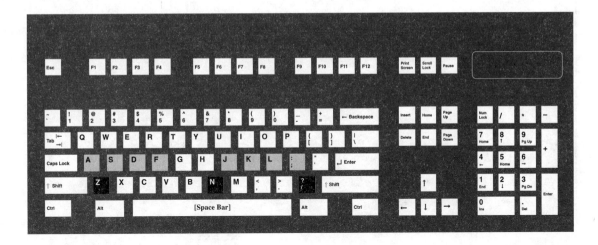

1. **Review:** Type each line twice. Double space after each 2-line group.

Line 4: Move F-finger from R to B; from B to T without pausing on home key.

```
abcd efgh ijkl mopq rstu vwxy abcd efgh ijkl mopq;
ark how eve box sue fly pad two hum jigs quit deck
A small boy with a watch has the time of his life.
verb verb verb curbs curbs curbs debts debts debts
much much much jumps jumps jumps rumor rumor rumor
```

Line 5: Move J-finger from M to U; from U to M without pausing on home key.

2. **New-Key Practice: Z** *Use A-Finger.*
   Practice the reach from **A** to **Z** and back home to **A.** Curl the finger as it reaches down to **Z.** Keep the **F**-finger in home position. When you can reach **Z** without looking at your fingers, type each line twice:

Fix each key location in your mind.

```
z z z z aza aza aza aza; zig zig zig; zag zag zag;
aza aza aza zip zip zip; zoo zoo zoo; zed zed zed;
aza aza aza adz adz adz; fiz fiz fiz; amaze amaze;
blitz blitz blitz; tizzy tizzy tizzy; craze craze;
viz., zest jazz lazy Zeke quiz whizz zebra zephyr;
```

3. **New-Key Practice: N** *Use J-Finger.*
   Practice the reach from **J** to **N** and back home to **J.** Keep the **K L ;** fingers in home position. When you can reach **N** without looking at your fingers, type each line twice:

All the alphabet keys.

```
n n n n jnj jnj jnj jnj; nil nil nil; sun sun sun;
jnj jnj jnj Ben Ben Ben; run run run; can can can;
jnj jnj jnj van van van; end end end; nix nix nix;
pen pen pen gun gun gun; now now now; ton ton ton;
won yen fun man gun hun din zinc junk links queen;
```

Move J-finger from U to N; from N to U without pausing on home key.

WORKS CITED

WORKS CITED

[1]Lindsell-Roberts, Sheryl L. *The Office Professional's Quick Reference Handbook.* (New York: Arco Publishing, 1995), p. 169.

[2]Hemphill, Phyllis David. *Business Communications with Writing Improvement Exercises.* (Englewood Cliffs: Prentice Hall, 1958), p. 146.

[3]Warriner, John and Sheila Y. Laws. *English Grammar and Communication.* (New York: Harcourt Brace Jovanovich, 1973), p. 22.

[4]Tuckman, Bruce W. *Conducting Educational Research.* 2d ed. (New York: Harcourt Brace Jovanovich, 1978), p. 15.

NOTE: This is a listing of all the works that have been cited and, as aforementioned, has replaced "footnotes." All the works cited should be listed in the order in which they are indicated in the text.

WORKS CONSULTED

WORKS CONSULTED

Bailey, Thomas A., *The Lusitania Disaster,* New York: The Free Press (division of Macmillan Publishing, Co., Inc.), 1975.

Cramer, Kenyon C., *The Cause of War,* Glenview, Ill.: Scott Foresman and Co., 1965.

Gray, Edwyn, *The Killing of Time: The U-Boat War 1914—1918,* New York: Charles Scribner's Sons, 1972.

May, Ernest, R., *The World War and American Isolation 1914—1917,* Cambridge, Mass.: Harvard University Press, 1966.

Millis, Walter, *Road to War: America, 1914—1917,* New York: Howard Fertig, Inc., 1970.

NOTE: The *Works Consulted* has replaced the bibliography. This is a listing of all sources of reference and starts two inches from the top of the page. It has one-inch side margins, and one tab indent (or five spaces) for runover lines. The format is the reverse of a paragraph.

All entries are in alphabetical order by author's last name.

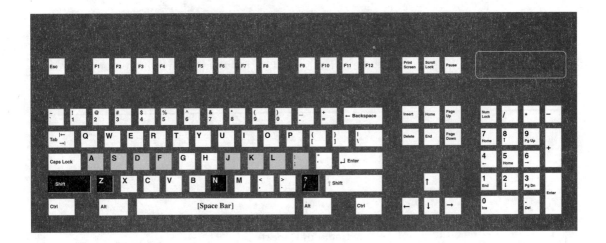

4. **New-Key Practice: ?** *Use ;-Finger.*

The **?** is on the /-key. Practice the reach like this: (1) Depress left shift key; (2) Reach for the /-key; (3) Move fingers back home. When you can do these 3 steps smoothly without looking at your fingers, type each line twice:

```
? ? ;?; ;?; ;?; Who? Who? Why? Why? Ben? Max? Vic?
Where is Zoel? Where is Marvin? Where is Robert?
```
Space once after ? at end of a sentence.

5. **Paragraph Practice:** Double Spaced.
Try for a PERFECT copy of each paragraph.

WORDS

All the alphabet keys.

```
    You want to do well in some subject. Why not      10
perfect your typing skill? You can use your skill     20
in many small ways to help you in your daily work.    30
     1    2    3    4    5    6    7    8    9    10
```

```
    You can also use your typing skill as a means     10
of securing an office job. It is a valuable skill     20
to have. You can acquire it; exert a bit of zeal.     30
     1    2    3    4    5    6    7    8    9    10
```

6. **Test Your Skill:** Take Three 1-Minute Timings.

GOAL: 15 words a minute within 3 errors.
Record your best speed within 3 errors.

Single-Spaced, Blocked Paragraph.
Set line spacing at "single."

WORDS

All the alphabet keys.

```
Mr. Querz: Joel Knox will get the xerox copies by     10
Tuesday. You will have five samples the same day.     20
     1    2    3    4    5    6    7    8    9    10
```

TITLE PAGE

Although many styles are acceptable, the title page generally contains the title of the report; the name of the person who prepared it; the office, school, or institution from which it originated; the date on which it was presented; and, in many cases, to whom it was presented.

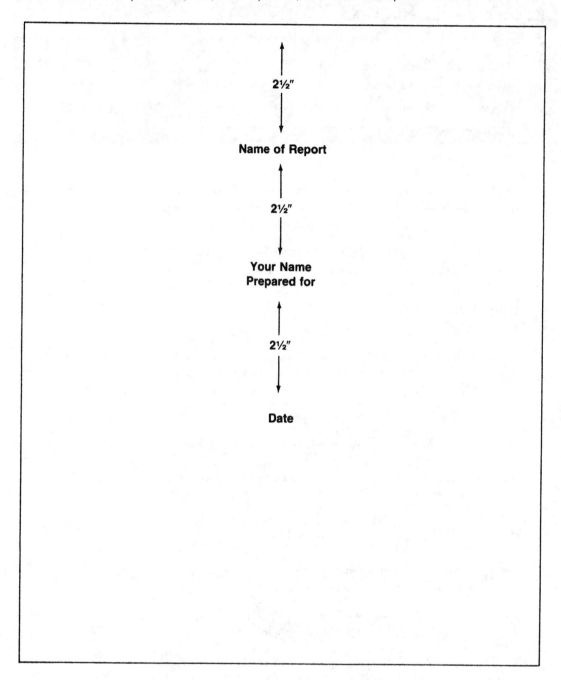

LESSON 12
- (Hyphen) Caps Lock

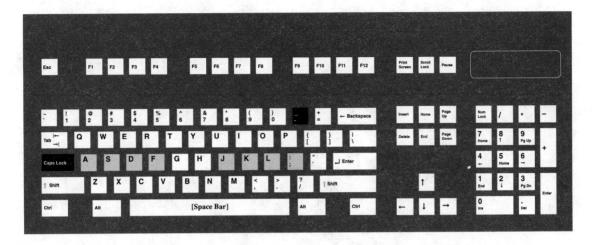

1. **Review:** Type each line twice. Double space after each 2-line group. The last line is easy. Practice it several times for speed. Start slowly, then g-r-a-d-u-a-l-l-y pick up speed as you go.

Home Row: `ask jal; ask a lad; half a glass; a lad had a fall`
First Row: `lax lax van van max max can can cab cabs jazz jazz`
Third Row: `wit yet ire ore type quit wrote erupt witty puppet`
Alphabet: `The quick brown fox jumped over the lazy old dogs.`
Speedup: `You can do the work well if you know how to do it.`
`    1    2    3    4    5    6    7    8    9    10`

Keep wrists low and relaxed but off the keyboard frame.

2. **New-Key Practice: - (Hyphen)** *Use ;-Finger.*
   Practice the reach from semicolon to hyphen and back home to semicolon. Straighten the **;**-finger as it goes up for the hyphen. Keep the **J**-finger in home position. When you can reach the hyphen without looking at your fingers, type each line twice:

All the alphabet keys.

`- - - ;-; ;-; ;-; ;-; one-half; one-half; one-half`
`;-; ;-; one-fifth; one-sixth; blue-gray; all-black`
`;-; ;-; zig-zag; part-time; half-price; by-product`
`;-; ;-; second-rate; son-in-law; up-to-date jacket`
`ice-clad; ready-made; quick-witted; vice-president`

No space before or after a hyphen.

3. **New-Key Practice: Caps Lock**
   To type words in all capitals, use the Caps Lock key. You could also choose "All caps" in font options.

LESSON 32
Manuscript Keyboarding

1. Spacing:

   A. Double space all lines.
   B. Indent all paragraphs one tab stop.

2. Margin Stops:

   Left and Right Margins: 1.25 inches on all pages

   Top Margin—Page 1

   2 inches

   Top Margin—Page 2
   and following pages

   1 inch

   Bottom Margin:
   1 inch on all pages

   A. Center the title in all capitals and/or underscore.
   B. Space down 3 single lines and start the first line in the copy. (If a cover page is used, these steps may be eliminated.)

3. Paragraph Headings:

   A. Space down 3 single lines from last typewritten line.
   B. Start the paragraph heading at the margin in all capitals.
   C. Double space and start paragraph.

4. Quotations

   3 lines or less:

   Type the quotation in the same paragraph—within quotation marks.

   4 lines or more:

   Type the quotation in a separate blocked paragraph without quotation marks. Use short lines, single spacing.

5. Page Numbers:

   Page numbering can be set as an automatic command. Refer to your user's manual.

6. Works Cited a/k/a
   Footnotes
   Works Consulted a/k/a
   Bibliography

   Footnotes and bibliographies seem to be going the way of the dinosaur. According to the *MLA [Modern Language Association] Handbook for Writers of Research Papers*, footnotes are now listed at the conclusion of a paper under the heading of "Works Cited." If you are including works that have been used for research and not necessarily cited, merely include them under the heading of "Works Consulted," the new term for bibliography.

These rules are illustrated by the models on the following pages.

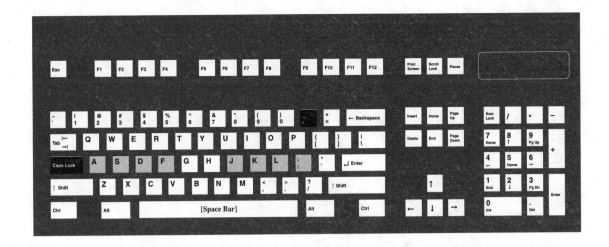

Type each line twice.

All the
alphabet
keys.

```
To type words in ALL CAPITALS, use the Caps Lock.
Zoel Buxton is now typing SMOOTHLY and ACCURATELY.
Dear Jacqueline: Who types FASTER, Max or Victor?
See the expert BOUNCE his THUMB off the space bar.
DEXTERITY in any skill comes from PROPER PRACTICE.
```

Release the Caps
Lock instantly after
you have typed the
word or words in ALL
CAPITALS.

4. **Paragraph Practice:** Single-Spaced, Blocked.
   Try for a PERFECT copy of each paragraph:

All the
alphabet
keys.

```
Dear Vera: I am glad to hear that your sister-in-
law passed the examination for high school teacher.
      1     2     3     4     5     6     7     8     9    10
```

Hyphen used to
combine words into a
"compound" word.

```
Dear Buzz: Did you know that Roxie Jimson--Shorty
to the class--won that school typewriting contest?
      1     2     3     4     5     6     7     8     9    10
```

Two hyphens used for
a dash. No space
before or after a dash.

NOTE: Another option is to use the em dash from the symbols screen.

5. **Test Your Skill:** Take Three 1-Minute Timings.

GOAL: 15 words a minute within 3 errors.
        Record your best speed within 3 errors.

WORDS

```
You can get there faster with push than with pull.    10
Time is money; so you must put it to the best use.    20
      1     2     3     4     5     6     7     8     9    10
```

The choice of a career is not an easy matter.	10
Tests cannot give a positive answer concerning the	20
career you should choose. You are too complex for	30
accurate and complete analysis. A test that shows	40
you are capable of doing a certain type of work is	50
no proof that you will be happy doing it. For the	60
choice of a career depends on a variety of factors.	70
The most important factors are your likes and	80
dislikes. So it seems you have to choose your own	90
career. No one can make the choice for you. Your	100
need for ready money might force you to accept the	110
first job offered. Such necessity should not kill	120
your drive to seek the kind of job you are set on.	130
You can still climb your way, little by little, to	140
that job. Make sure your choice is an intelligent	150
one. Then equip yourself for that sort of career.	160

1   2   3   4   5   6   7   8   9   10

LESSON 13
1 3 7

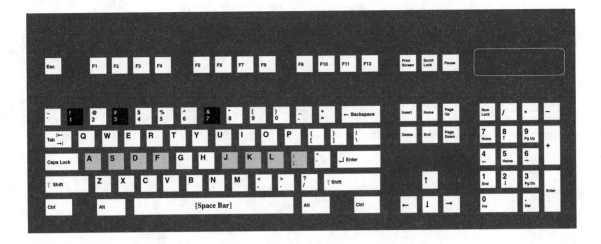

1. **Review:** Type each line twice. Double space after each 2-line group.

Alphabet: abc cde efg ghi ijk klm mno opq qrs stu uvwx xyzab
A: and aid ale; ant all air; apt ace ark; act age aim
B: bit boy but; beg bid bow; box bar bib; beg bin bob
(Hyphen): ;-; ;-; ;-; zig-zag; re-enter; part-time; one-half
Speedup: Why did we not pay that man who did all that work?

        1   2   3   4   5   6   7   8   9   10

NOTE: When you are entering numbers, you have the option of the standard keyboard or numeric pad. The numeric pad is especially useful to anyone who is used to performing numeric calculations on a calculator-type keypad. To use the numeric pad, be certain the "Num Lock" key is activated. Many keyboards will display a light above the pad letting you know that number lock is activated. Consider doing the following exercises on the standard keyboard and numeric pad.

2. **New-Key Practice: 1**
   If you have a **1** key on the top row, use **A**-finger.
   If you have no **1** key, type the small **L** for **1.**
   Type each line twice:

   ala ala ala ala Add 1 and 1 and 11 and 11 and 111.
   11 acts 11 apes 11 axes 11 lads 11 loads 11 lamps;
   Cal will be 1 year and 11 months old next June 11.
   We need 11 pairs of size 11 socks for the 11 boys.
   Bus No. 11 on Route 11 is due to arrive in 1 hour.

   Relax your shoulders. Let your arms hang loosely at your sides.

If you go into a store and buy things without   10

paying cash for them, you are said to be buying on   20

credit; that is, in lieu of paying cash you pledge   30

to pay for the goods at some future time. A great   40

many big firms do business on an all-credit basis.   50

The free use of credit has grown into a very   60

important factor in our business life today. It   70

is said that people who buy on credit in our land   80

now owe many billions of dollars for things which   90

they bought on time, or for money which they have   100

borrowed. About a third of the money owed is for   110

these goods: cars, radios, TV sets, and furniture.   120

Why has credit been used so often in business   130

life? It's thought that most individuals who buy   140

on credit see in credit the only way they can get   150

all the goods they desire but cannot pay in cash.   160

    1   2   3   4   5   6   7   8   9   10

Lesson 31: Mastery Drills and Timed Tests

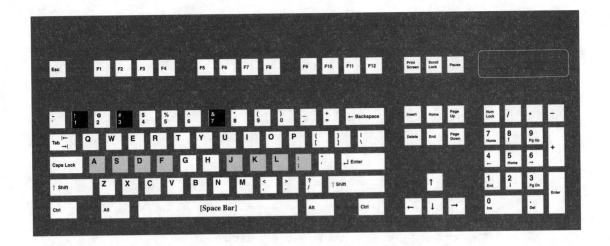

3. **New-Key Practice: 3** *Use D-Finger.*
   Practice the reach from **D** to **3** and back home to **D**. Keep the **F**-finger at home. When you can reach **3** without looking at your fingers, type each line twice:

```
3 3 3 d3d d3d d3d 3 and 31 and 113 and 131 and 313
3 days 3 dogs 3 dads; 33 dolls 33 dishes 33 dukes;
Donald and his 3 pals caught 13 fish on August 31.
For the next quiz, read pages 3, 13, 31, 131, 133.
Ben Cox will be 13 years 3 months old December 31.
```

Think of the finger and the number it controls.

4. **New-Key Practice: 7** *Use J-Finger.*
   Practice the reach from **J** to **7** and back home to **J**. Keep the semicolon-finger at home. When you can reach **7** without looking at your fingers, type each line twice:

```
7 7 7 j7j j7j j7j 7 and 17 and 37 and 173 and 317;
7 jugs 7 jars 7 jewels 17 jeeps 37 jokes 137 jobs;
17 John Street; 37 James Avenue; 137 Jackson Blvd.
Of the 37 students, 17 typed at 13 words a minute.
What is the sum of 1 and 7 and 13 and 173 and 371?
```

Stretch finger to a top-row key.

5. **Paragraph Practice:** Double Spacing.
   Try for 2 PERFECT copies of this paragraph:

WORDS

```
  It is easy to type the figures 1 and 3 and 7.          10

It is even easy to mix these figures and type such      20

numbers as 317, 173, 371, 713, 137, 171, 737, 373.     30
      1     2     3     4     5     6     7     8     9    10
```

Anyone who can read can learn to read faster.	10
You do not need a keen mind for reading speed. An	20
education helps but if you have a fairly extensive	30
vocabulary, then you do not need formal education.	40
The slow readers have a habit of reading word	50
by word; they devote full attention to every word.	60
They should, instead, look only for the meaning of	70
groups of words. What you really want in all your	80
reading is the author's idea. The words he or she	90
uses are not important. Many words can be cut out	100
of a piece of writing without loss of the meaning.	110
So get the habit of reading solely for ideas.	120
You will then see that you are taking in groups of	130
words at a glance and that you are reading faster.	140
To help you keep in mind what you read, train your	150
mind to see the way the author presents the ideas.	160

    1   2   3   4   5   6   7   8   9   10

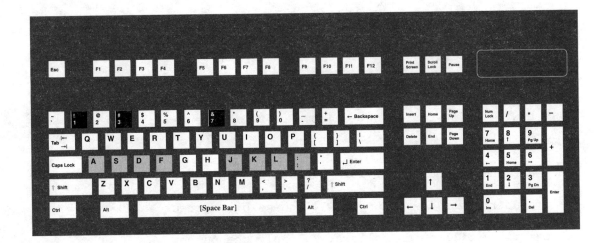

6. **Test Your Skill:** Take Three 2-Minute Timings.

Follow these steps in all your 2-minute timings.

A. Repeat if you finish before end of 2 minutes.

B. After each timing, jot down total words typed and total errors. Practice the words that have errors till they are easy for you.

C. Your 2-minute speed is words typed divided by 2.

EXAMPLE: 23 words ÷ 2 = 11½ = 12 words a minute.

D. Record on your Progress Chart (page 136) your best speed within 4 errors.

GOAL: 18 words a minute within 4 errors.

WORDS

```
 Fix your mind on what you are typing. Start       10

at a slow pace and gradually work up to your best  20

speed. Do not type so fast that you lose control.  30

Typing speed grows like a baby--slowly, gradually. 40
```
        1   2   3   4   5   6   7   8   9   10

Do you enjoy magic tricks? Here is one trick   10

you will enjoy trying out on some of your friends: 20

Ask the friend to jot down his age on a piece   30

of paper; then say that you will guess his correct   40

age if he will do as follows: Multiply the number   50

by two and add four to the answer. Then, multiply   60

by three and divide by six. Ask to see the number   70

your friend now has. Subtract two from the number   80

and you will then tell the person his correct age.   90

Example: The person's age is 19. Ask him or her   100

to multiply it by 2; that makes it 38; 38 plus   110

4 is 42; 42 times 3 is 126; 126 divided by 6 is 21;   120

21 minus 2 is age 19. Try to memorize these steps   130

exactly. It would spoil the fun to read them from   140

a memo. The trick works with any number selected.   150

     1   2   3   4   5   6   7   8   9   10

LESSON 14
2 6

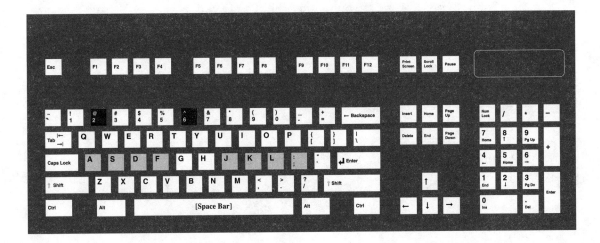

1. **Review:** Type each line twice. Double space after each 2-line group.

Alphabet: The quiz Jay picked for six big men will vex them.
1 3 7: Type these numbers: 13 17 71 137 317 373 713 173.
C: cot cub cab; cop cow cur; cat can cup; cob coy cad
D: did due dad; dip die dab; day din dye; dew dun dog
Speedup: The man will be paid if he fills out the pay form.

```
     1    2    3    4    5    6    7    8    9    10
```

Return to the margin quickly without looking up.

2. **New-Key Practice: 2** *Use S-Finger.*
   Practice the reach from **S** to **2** and back home to **S.** Try to keep the **F**-finger in home position. When you can reach **2** without looking at your fingers, type each line twice:

   2 2 2 s2s s2s s2s 2 steps 2 seals 2 shops 2 stones
   2 ships 2 sails 2 sizes 2 skirts 2 shapes 2 spaces
   June 27, 1232; September 12, 1272; August 23, 1322
   Cora Dix will be 12 years 2 months old January 27.
   Add these figures: 2, 12, 21, 23, 27, 32, and 72.

   Space once after a colon.

3. **New-Key Practice: 6** *Use J-Finger.*
   Practice the reach from **J** to **6** and back home to **J.** Stretch the **J**-finger up and to the left. Keep the **;**-finger home. When you can reach **6** without looking at your fingers, type each line twice:

   6 6 6 j6j j6j j6j 6 jumps 6 jails 6 jeeps 6 jests;
   6 jades 6 jaunts 6 jacks 6 juries 6 jewels 6 jobs;
   August 6, 1627; October 3, 1632; November 12, 1766
   What is the sum of 21 and 63 and 27 and 16 and 26?
   Maxie paid 62 cents for 16 stamps he used June 26.

In olden times, long, long ago, there lived a   10

king named Midas. He lived in a beautiful palace.   20

He had a pretty wife and a pretty daughter whom he   30

dearly loved, and lots of money to buy everything.   40

Yet this king was not happy. He was a miser.   50

He loved money for its own sake. In a secret room   60

in his palace he kept all his gold. He spent each   70

day counting over and over again his golden hoard.   80

One day he asked the Greek god named Dionysus   90

to grant him the wish of his life--that everything   100

he touched might turn to gold; and it was granted.   110

But King Midas, when he saw even his food changed   120

to gold, had to beg the god to take his gift back.   130

The story of King Midas is a myth, a fanciful   140

tale that has come down to us from many ages past.   150

    1   2   3   4   5   6   7   8   9   10

Lesson 31: Mastery Drills and Timed Tests   **100**

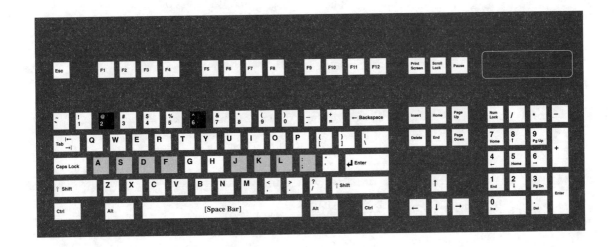

4. **Paragraph Practice:** Double Spacing.
   Try for a PERFECT copy of each paragraph:

WORDS

One space
between a
whole
number and
a "made"
fraction.

You can easily make fractions by using the /.   10

Try typing the following few examples: 2/3, 1/6,   20

6/7, 1/3, 3/16, 2 1/7, 6 2/3, 3 6/7, 2 1/6, 7 1/12   30

    1   2   3   4   5   6   7   8   9   10

NOTE: When you create a fraction using the slash, some programs will automatically convert it to a single-character fraction. (Example: 1/2 becomes $\frac{1}{2}$.)

WORDS

Business typists use the / to shorten certain   10

terms in invoices. For example, they type B/L for   20

Bill of Lading: A/C for Account; N/C for No Charge   30

    1   2   3   4   5   6   7   8   9   10

All the
alphabet
keys plus all
the numbers
you know.

Maxie, Buzz, and Vicki read pages 26, 31, and   10

62; they worked out problems 2, 6, 37, and 62 just   20

in time to hand them to Prof. Quimby before class.   30

Maxie, Buzz, and Vicki are pals and work together.   40

    1   2   3   4   5   6   7   8   9   10

Lesson 14: 2 6

You want a place in which to live, the proper   10

food, clothing, and all the other things that make   20

for comfort and convenience and life worth living.   30

But all the things you desire you cannot have just   40

for the asking. You simply have to work for them.   50

Yet, at one time each family had to depend on   60

its own effort for all the things it needed. Each   70

family made its own clothing, raised its own food,   80

and put aside a sufficient surplus for the winter.   90

Now, each person makes a living by performing   100

special work for which he or she is paid in money.   110

With this money we all can get the things we need.   120

    1   2   3   4   5   6   7   8   9   10

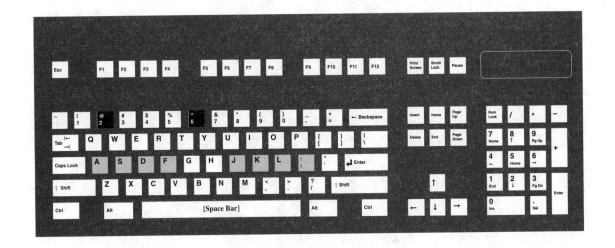

5. **Test Your Skill:** Take Three 2-Minute Timings.

GOAL: 18 words a minute within 4 errors.
Record your best speed within 4 errors.

WORDS

Use double
spacing.

If you type well, you can put your ideas down   10

on paper just as fast as they pop up in your mind.   20

You will gain this goal if you put forth your best   30

efforts in your daily lesson. Learn to type well.   40

    1   2   3   4   5   6   7   8   9   10

Money's the best gift; it's easy to exchange.	10
The love of money is a love which never grows old.	20
Money is what you use if you have no credit cards.	30
The trouble with money is that it favors the rich.	40
Anybody with cold cash gets a warm reception.	50
What gives money its value is the work you put in.	60
Some folks never think of money--when they owe it.	70
Money talks but it does so only with the very few.	80
Money will be our best friend in our old age.	90
Money makes the car go and the car makes money go.	100
Money is mighty but can't make a dog wag its tail.	110
A dollar would go farther if it didn't go so fast.	120

1   2   3   4   5   6   7   8   9   10

LESSON 15
5 9

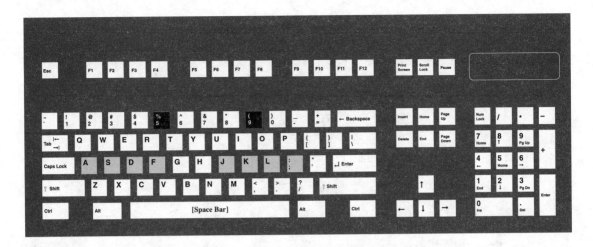

1. **Review:** Type each line twice. Double space after each 2-line group.

Alphabet: very buzz stew code flax ruse high main joke quips
1 2 3 6 7: What is the sum of 12 and 16 and 37 and 73 and 62?
E: end ere egg; eel eke ebb; elk eve eat; ewe elf eye
F: fib fog fit; fox fop fur; fat few fun; fig fed fix
Speedup: The old man does good work and is fit for the job.

    1   2   3   4   5   6   7   8   9   10

Use the correct finger for each number.

2. **New-Key Practice: 5** *Use F-Finger.*
   Practice the reach from **F** to **5** and back home to **F.** Keep the **A**-finger at home. When you can reach **5** without looking at your fingers, type each line twice:

   5 5 5 f5f f5f f5f 5 flags 5 flaps 5 fires 55 files
   5 figs 5 fish 5 flew 5 fads 5 fix 5 fled 55 frames
   Of the 25 students, 16 typed at 37 words a minute.
   On June 1, there were 35 big ships in Fleet No. 5.
   The correct answer to problem 52 is 5^3/s exactly.

No. is the abbreviation for number. Space once after an abbreviation.

3. **New-Key Practice: 9** *Use L-Finger.*
   Practice the reach from **L** to **9** and back home to **L.** Try to keep the **J**-finger at home. When you can reach **9** without looking at your fingers, type each line twice:

   9 9 9 191 191 191 9 lamps 9 loads 9 lambs 9 ladies
   9 lids 9 legs 9 laws 9 lots 9 laps 9 lads 9 lights
   Only 16 of the 59 typists made final grades of 95.
   What is the sum of 19 and 25 and 36 and 73 and 95?
   At 9:15 a.m., May 9, I flew to Paris on Flight 59.

No space after period between small initials.

You may have heard about Diogenes, a wise man	10
of ancient Greece. On one occasion he walked down	20
many streets of his home town at midday carrying a	30
lighted lantern. When he was asked to account for	40
such strange conduct, he said that he was out just	50
looking for an honest man.	55
Folks started to laugh and shake their heads.	65
They thought there was surely something wrong with	75
him. But, of course, we all now know he was sane.	85
He simply tried to dramatize the fact that honesty	95
in his day was a rare virtue. Even now in our own	105
day and age it seems this virtue is not yet common.	115

1   2   3   4   5   6   7   8   9   10

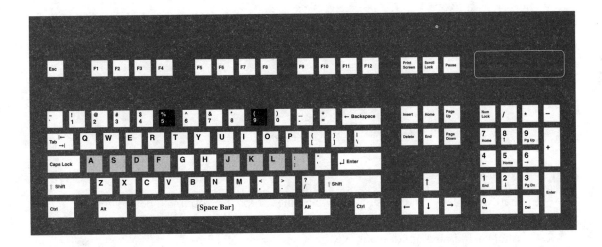

4. **Paragraph Practice:** Double Spacing.
   Try for 2 PERFECT copies of this note:

	WORDS
Dear Zoel:	2

All the alphabet keys plus all the numbers you know.

	WORDS
Up to now, I sold 9 tickets for the August 25	12
game. Val Fox and Joe Quin sold 17; Pat, 16; Ben,	22
13; and Cy, 12. This makes a total of 67 tickets.	32
Tell coach Yardley that we are ahead of our quota.	42

     1   2   3   4   5   6   7   8   9   10

5. **Test Your Skill:** Take Three 2-Minute Timings.

   GOAL: 18 words a minute within 4 errors.
         Record your best speed within 4 errors.

	WORDS
When a student finally steps into the working	10
world, he or she finds that the boss is a lot more	20
exact in a host of matters than were those patient	30
and kind teachers all liked so much at the school.	40

     1   2   3   4   5   6   7   8   9   10

5-MINUTE TIMED TESTS
(Pages 97 to 104)

Before You Take a Test:

1. Clear the screen.
2. Set margins to 1".
3. Double space.

Test Procedure: (Take one test a day.)

1. Start with Test 1. Take three 5-minute timings. Repeat if you finish before end of 5 minutes.
2. After each timing, jot down total words typed and total errors.
3. Practice the words that have errors until they are easy for you.
4. Select your best speed within 5 errors.

Score Your Tests:

1. Use the Progress Chart for Timings on page 136.
2. Set your goal: 5 words a minute higher than your present speed.
3. Record your best speed in Test 1. With Test 2, start joining the scores and watch your progress.
4. If you reach your goal before Test 8, set a new goal at 5 words a minute higher than before. Start over again with Test 1.

Skill-Booster Tips:

1. Curve fingers slightly; hold them as close as possible to home keys without touching the keys. Tap the keys very lightly.
2. Move the fingers only. Try not to move wrists, elbows, arms.
3. Keep your eyes on the copy at all times.
4. Speed up the shift-key stroke. Do it in a continuous 1-2-3 motion: ONE, depress shift key. TWO, hold it down while you strike the correct key. THREE, release shift key, move finger back home.
5. Type evenly and smoothly.
6. Type short, common words like *the, had,* without spelling them (t h e) (h a d). Flash them as a unit (the) (had).
7. Fix your mind only on the work you are doing.
8. To help you avoid frequent errors on certain letters, figures, or symbols, practice the appropriate Mastery Drills on pages 92 and 93.

LESSON 16
4 8 0

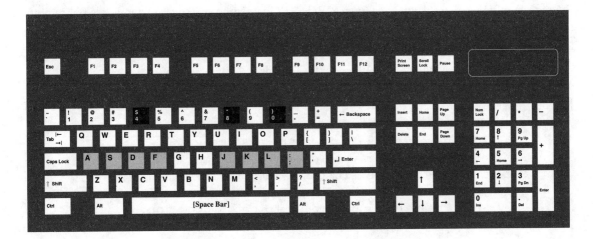

1. **Review:** Type each line twice. Double space after each 2-line group.

Alphabet: Haste is waste. Take it easy. Life is too short.
1 2 3 5 6 7 9: Order 35 pads, 169 erasers, 236 pens, 327 pencils.
G: get gob gut; gal gap gum; gig gag gun; gas gin god
H: hoe hop hum; hit had hut; him her hex; hew hen hog
Speedup: The old man who does good work will get a day off.

       1   2   3   4   5   6   7   8   9   10

Try to start each line without a pause.

2. **New-Key Practice: 4** *Use F-Finger.*
   Practice the reach from **F** to **4** and back home to **F.** Keep the **A**-finger at home. When you can reach **4** without looking at your fingers, type each line twice:

   4 4 4 f4f f4f f4f 4 flaps 4 flags 4 fires 4 firms;
   4 figs 4 furs 4 fish 4 files 4 facts 4 farms 144.4
   About 44 boys took the 14-mile hike June 14, 1944.
   Add these figures: 4 and 14 and 49 and 64 and 74.
   The 14 boys caught the 4:15 p.m. train on Track 4.

3. **New-Key Practice: 8** *Use K-Finger.*
   Practice the reach from **K** to **8** and back home to **K.** Keep **;**-finger in home position. When you can reach **8** without looking at your fingers, type each line twice:

   8 8 8 k8k k8k k8k 8 knots 8 knobs 8 kites 8 kinds;
   8 keys 8 kings 8 kits 8 kids 8 kegs 8 killed 48.14
   What is the sum of 8 and 48 and 84 and 88 and 418?
   The 84 men worked a total of 484 hours on July 18.
   Vince will call tomorrow at 8:15 A.M. or 4:15 P.M.

Space once after period following capital initials.

SPEED BOOSTERS

One good way to boost your speed is to type easy sentences over and over. They help you type smoothly without pausing.

Practice each sentence until you can type it PERFECTLY in the time you select. Your words-per-minute speed is given under that time.

Time in Seconds:	15	30	45	60
Words-per-Minute:	40	20	13	10

WORDS: 1   2   3   4   5   6   7   8   9   10

1. Try to do your work just as well as you can do it.
2. Many a true word is said in jest; also many a lie.
3. Aim for the top; it may help you to land half way.
4. Mama and papa must be fit for a baby to live with.
5. In days of yore they who did not work did not eat.
6. They who type well find it easy to get a good job.
7. You must hand it to the tax man or he may take it.
8. The boss will find out if you do good work or not.
9. A man with a bald head is one who came out on top.
10. If at the end of the rope, tie a knot and hang on.
11. Your car is out of date as soon as it is paid for.
12. The law of life: You must work for what you wish.
13. If you skip a meal, you are sure to eat with zest.
14. Know your job; that is the way to make good at it.
15. Life is a game; play to win--and ever with a grin.
16. All can take a day off but no one can put it back.
17. Eat it all but chew each bite ere you let it fall.
18. Guys who do not win fair lady know not how to woo.
19. Most all men are good--as good as they have to be.
20. All work and no play robs one of some fun in life.

    1   2   3   4   5   6   7   8   9   10

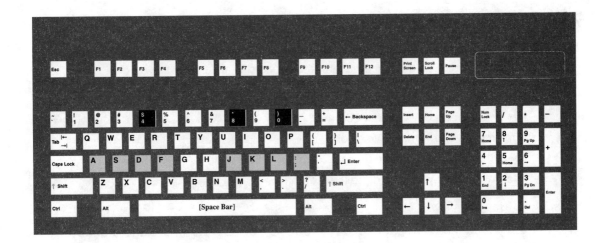

4. **New-Key Practice: 0** *Use ;-Finger.*
   Practice the reach from **;** to **0** and back home to **;**. Keep the **J**-finger at home. Keep elbow close to body. When you can reach **0** without looking at your fingers, type each line twice.

   ```
   0 0 0 ;0; ;0; ;0; 10 pins 10 pals 10 pads 10 packs
   10 pets 10 pews 10 pegs 10 plums 10 plays 10 plans
   The teams will practice at 10:30 a.m. or 2:30 p.m.
   There were 150 to 170 men at the March 10 meeting.
   Buzzy is 10 years 10 months and 10 days old today.
   ```

5. **Paragraph Practice:** Double Spacing.
   Try for 2 PERFECT copies of this note:

		WORDS

The whole alphabet and all the numbers.

```
Dear Walt:                                              2

   I have arranged to have the Annual Banquet of       12

The Commercial Club meet at the Duke Hotel on June     22

9 at 8:00 p.m. in Room 1364. I expect at least 25      32

of our members to attend. Please manage to return      42

all unsold tickets to Mr. Zims by Tuesday, June 7.     52
        1    2    3    4    5    6    7    8    9    10
```

ALPHABETIC SENTENCES

Alphabetic sentences give you a thorough review of all the letters; they help you to gain perfect control of the keyboard. Type them at an even, steady pace, as accurately as you can.

Follow this routine:

1. Try a sentence a day—type it 10 times.
2. Practice the words that have errors.
3. Type the sentence 10 more times.
4. Start over when you have done them all.

WORDS: 1   2   3   4   5   6   7   8   9   10   11   12

1. Jerry and Martha packed five dozen quilts in two huge boxes.
2. Felix Quope and Zeb Graves may cause a fire with their junk.
3. A showy trapeze artist quickly jumped over five green boxes.
4. That quip lazy Dick made about Jackie vexed a few neighbors.
5. Jack Pahlevy of Iraq found two big azure boxes of marijuana.
6. Jovial chemist Grub quickly froze a mixture of brown powder.
7. A lazy witness from Quebec vexed patient judge Walter Kache.
8. Jacqueline Wytbok purchased several fur rugs in mixed sizes.
9. Two big foxes quickly jumped over those lazy, sleeping dogs.
10. Paul Van Weems, an expert glazier, quickly finished the job.
11. The hazard of quack medicines will be exposed by Dr. Juvtig.
12. Cy Jexon, a brainy wag, quickly solved the fish maze puzzle.
13. They quizzed four experts about knowledge of juvenile crime.
14. Macy will pack my box with five dozen jugs of liquid veneer.
15. Hy Quiveg will systematize complex jobs and jack up profits.
16. Marvin quickly packed the box with five dozen jugs for Iraq.
17. Many extra quick flights to Brazil uncovered perfect jewels.
18. Cy and Elza did mix the big jar of soapy water very quickly.
19. Five pale gray taxis whizzed by the Jonquin Steamship docks.
20. Max Vidjub zips fingers quickly across keys without pausing.

1   2   3   4   5   6   7   8   9   10   11   12

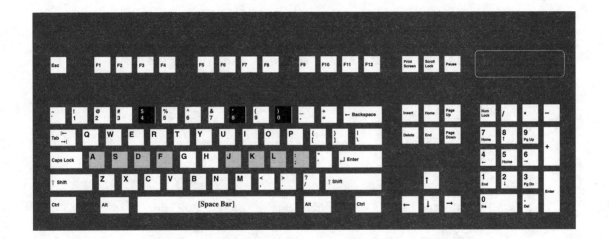

6. **Test Your Skill:** Take Three 2-Minute Timings.

GOAL: 18 words a minute within 4 errors.
Record your best speed within 4 errors.

WORDS

Use double
spacing.

You will not learn much that counts if you do   10

not have the urge to learn. This is a thought you   20

may well ponder. Always strive to equip yourself   30

with the necessary skills to excel in your career.   40

   1   2   3   4   5   6   7   8   9   10

Number Keys

1	a1a a1a a1a aq1 aq1 1 lass 1 light 1 apple 1 quart
2	sw2 sw2 s2s s2s s2s 2 sets 2 sales 2 sacks 2 ships

3	de3 de3 d3d d3d d3d 3 dads 3 deals 3 dukes 3 drugs
4	fr4 fr4 f4f f4f f4f 4 furs 4 firms 4 flags 4 fires

5	fr5 fr5 f5f f5f f5f 5 feet 5 fines 5 files 5 farms
6	jy6 jy6 j6j j6j j6j 6 jobs 6 jeeps 6 jokes 6 jails

7	ju7 ju7 j7j j7j j7j 7 jugs 7 jumps 7 jokes 7 jacks
8	ki8 ki8 k8k k8k k8k 8 kits 8 kinds 8 kicks 8 kites

9	109 109 191 191 191 9 lads 9 lamps 9 lives 9 locks
10	;p0 ;p0 ;0; ;0; ;0; 10 pay 10 put 10 pals 10 pints

Symbol/Special Keys

$	f$f f$f f$f f$f Give her $40 or $41 or $42 or $43.
&	j&j j&j j&j j&j Macy & Web; Zale & Quig; Dix & Co.

%	f%f f%f f%f f%f I got 25%; Cy got 35%; Al got 40%.
#	d#d d#d d#d d#d We need 73# of #38 and 63# of #39.

( )	1(1 1(1 ;); ;); (one) (two) (three) (four) (five);
:	;:; ;:; ;:; Dear Al: Dear Hy: Dear Jo: Dear Ma:

?	;?; ;?; ;?; He? Who? Why? When? Which? Where?
/	;/; ;/; ;/; a/c d/c n/c c/o and/or we/they 2/3 5/8

Practice the following drills.

__	j__j j__j j__j j__j We <u>must</u> have <u>all the copies</u> today.
	;__; ;__; ;__; ;__; Your money is <u>refunded</u> in <u>10 days</u>.

@	;@; ;@; ;@; bags @ $20; boxes @ $30; cartons @ $90
	s@s s@s s@s bags @ $23; boxes @ $25; cartons @ $28

"	s"s s"s s"s s"s "wow" "sow" "slow" "show" "straw";
	;"; ;"; ;"; ;"; "pep" "pup" "plop" "prop" "plump";

'	k'k k'k k'k Dick's coat; Dick's scarf; Dick's pin;
	;'; ;'; ;'; Hap's tires; Hap's auto; Hap's garage;

*	;*; ;*; ;*; ;*; Sale lots are marked *; as 10* 20* 30*
	k*k k*k k*k k*k Sale lots are marked *; as 48* 58* 68*

LESSON 17
$ (Dollars) ' (Apostrophe)

1. **Review:** Type each line twice. Double space after each 2-line group.

Good posture helps
you to avoid errors.

Alphabet: `feed back soap high flux over quit jazz many words`
All Numbers: `Type these numbers: 1929, 1934, 1947, 1968, 1985`
I: `ill ice inn; ilk ire icy; ink imp Ida; Ina Ivy Ike`
J: `jam jag joy; joe jug job; jud jig jab; Jan Jay Joy`
Speedup: `That farm work is too hard for old men to do well.`
        `1    2    3    4    5    6    7    8    9    10`

2. **New-Key Practice: $** *Use F-Finger.*
    The **$** is on the **4**-key. (1) Depress right shift key; (2) Reach for the **4**-key; (3) Move fingers back home. When you can do these 3 steps smoothly without looking at your fingers, type each line twice:

No space
between the
sign $ and a
number.

`$ $ $ f$f f$f f$f Give $40 or $41, not $45 or $46.`
`f$f f$f f$f Get the jar for $4; the jug for $4.50.`
`f$f f$f f$f Buy the jalopy for $400, not for $475.`
`My bill is $446. My check is for $442. I owe $4.`
`The diamond costs $450; the pearl, $40; send $490.`

3. **New-Key Practice: '(Apostrophe)**

Use
apostrophe
to indicate:
1. Ownership
2. Contraction
3. Feet

A. The **'** is beside the **;**-key. Use the **;**-finger. Practice the reach from **;** to **'** and back home to **;**. Keep the **J**-finger at home. When you can reach the **'** without looking at your fingers, type this drill twice:

`` ` ` ` ;'; ;'; ;'; It is Kip's job to fix Hap's car. ``

B. Type each line twice:

No space before or
after an apostrophe
within a word.

`Hello Suzy: Max saw Vicki's car in Jack's garage.`
`Ben couldn't wear Frank's hat; it wasn't his size.`
`Dixie is 4 3/4' tall; her brother Quill is 5 1/2'.`
`Don't pay $9 for the pin! It isn't worth so much!`
`Marvin, you've done a good job! I'm proud of you!`

LESSON 31
MASTERY DRILLS AND TIMED TESTS

To help you master the keyboard, list the keys on which you often make errors. Then practice the drill for each key until you can type it smoothly and accurately.

Alphabet Keys

A	aa aAa alarms animal appear attain awaken aa aAa
B	bb bBb babble bribes bubble barber blurbs bb bBb
C	cc cCc circus circle cracks cactus clutch cc cCc
D	dd dDd dawdle addled delude deride divide dd dDd
E	ee eEe evenly events evolve energy emerge ee eEe
F	ff fFf fifths fluffs fluffy offers suffer ff fFf
G	gg gGg groggy gauges goggle gargle giggle gg gGg
H	hh hHh health height hyphen hushed higher hh hHh
I	ii iIi idioms idiots inning incite invite ii iIi
J	jj jJj jalopy juggle junior jejune jujube jj jJj
K	kk kKk kicker knacks knocks kulaks kopeck kk kKk
L	ll lLl lilies lulled loller lolled llamas ll lLl
M	mm mMm mimics maxims maimed mammal mammon mm mMm
N	nn nNn ninety nonage noncom nation Newton nn nNn
O	oo oOo oppose oozing onions oblong odious oo oOo
P	pp pPp pepsin pepper papers poplin poplar pp pPp
Q	qq qQq quirks quacks quaint qualms quarry qq qQq
R	rr rRr rumors rivers repair rarely return rr rRr
S	ss sSs shirts sleeps shreds sister series ss sSs
T	tt tTt tattle taunts taught tattoo tatter tt tTt
U	uu uUu usurer usurps future upturn Ursula uu uUu
V	vv vVv valves velvet vivify vervet devolve vv vVv
W	ww wWw winnow widows window willow wallow ww wWw
X	xx xXx exerts taxing X-rays Xerxes boxing xx xXx
Y	yy yYy yeasty yellow yearly yonder yachts yy yYy
Z	zz zZz sizzle guzzle zigzag buzzer pizzas zz zZz

4. **Paragraph Practice:** Double Spacing.
   Try for a PERFECT copy of each paragraph.

WORDS

Here is what it cost us to put our men on the   10

moon: $1.1 billion for research; $3.3 billion for   20

designing; $9.4 billion for Saturn Rocket Engines;   30

$7.8 billion for spacecraft; and $2.25 billion for   40

salaries to scientists, office supplies, and help.   50

Total cost of the moon flight: about $24 billion.   60

   1   2   3   4   5   6   7   8   9   10

WORDS

Christopher must catch the bus at 7:30 sharp.   10

He attends St. Michael's School at 47 Bonnie Brown   20

Avenue. He rides the bus with Chrissy and Willie.   30

To succeed you must work hard at what you do.   40

When the going gets rough, breathe deep and go on.   50

Pick yourself up, think of a good thing, be happy.   60

   1   2   3   4   5   6   7   8   9   10

5. **Test Your Skill:** Take Three 3-Minute Timings.
   Follow these steps in all your 3-minute timings.

   A. Repeat if you finish before the end of 3 minutes.
   B. After each timing, jot down total words typed and total errors. Practice the words that have errors until they are easy for you.
   C. Your 3-minute speed is words typed divided by 3.
   D. Record on your Progress Chart (page 136) your best speed within 4 errors.

   GOAL: 20 words a minute within 4 errors.

6. Generate this numbered list automatically.

    Let's consider the following items at the meeting:

    1. Next year's production schedule
    2. The year-end fiscal report
    3. The five-year corporate plan

The mature person bears the accidents of life	10
with grace and dignity, making the best of things.	20
Your mind is like your stomach; it is not how	30
much you put into it, but how much you can digest.	40
The value of an education lies in the ability	50
to make a living out of the know-how you acquired.	60

1   2   3   4   5   6   7   8   9   10

LESSON 30
Borders, Shading, Bulleted Lists, and Numbered Lists

Have a little fun with your computer. Refer to your user's manual and try to copy these exercises.

1. Type this text and center it. Put a shadow box border around it.

> Never explain. Your friends do not need it and your
> enemies will not believe you anyway.
>
> —Elbert Hubbard, American Writer

2. Type this text and align to the right. Put a $^3/_4$ pt. double-line border around it.

> An acronym is a word that's derived from its initials. For example, OPEC
> (Organization of Petroleum Exporting Countries) is an acronym.
> FBI (Federal Bureau of Investigation) is an initialism.

3. Type this text and align to the left. Put a $^3/_4$ pt. double-line border with a shadow box around it.

> The world is full of color. We use color to define much of what we see. Color adds
> visual impact. It allows us to separate the ripe from the unripe and the light from the
> dark. Using color in your documents will give the documents a real-world look.

4. Type this text and center it. Put 5% shading around it.

> There was a sign in a hotel in Zurich, Switzerland, which read: "Because of the
> impropriety of entertaining guests of the opposite sex in the bedroom, it is suggested
> that the lobby be used for this purpose.

5. Generate this bulleted list automatically.

   Use a numbered list

   • to show priorities

   • to show steps in a procedure

   • for items that have been quantified

   • for easy reference

LESSON 18
(Number or Pounds)
& (Ampersand)

1. **Review:** Type each line twice. Double space after each 2-line group.

Alphabet: `Jack Quigly packed my truck with five dozen boxes.`   Eyes on copy. Be a
$/`;`: `f4$ f$f $8.20 $13 ' ' ' ;'; This is Joe's sweater.`   touch typist.
K: `kit key kale; kat kip kay; ken keep keel; keg kick`
L: `lap lot leg; lab lax law; lid lug lay; low let lip`
Speedup: `When you take a job, your duty is to do good work.`

```
    1     2     3     4     5     6     7     8     9     10
```

2. **New-Key Practice: #** The # is on the **3**-key. *Use D-Finger.*
Practice the reach like this: (1) Depress the right shift key; (2) Reach for the **3**-key; (3) Move fingers back home. When you can do these 3 steps without looking at your fingers, type each line twice:

No space
between the
sign # and a
number.

```
# # # d#d d#d d#d Ship Orders #30, #35, #37, #383.
d#d d#d d#d Pay Bills #3, #31, #32, #36, #38, #39.
Pack these in lots of 10#, 29#, 38#, 56#, and 74#.
d3d d3# d#d d#d The sign # means number or pounds.
We shipped 13# of #310 and 53# of #37 to the firm.
```

3. **New-Key Practice: &** The & is on the **7**-key. *Use J-Finger.*
Practice the reach like this: (1) Depress the left shift key; (2) Reach for the **7**-key; (3) Move fingers back home. When you can do these 3 steps without looking at your fingers, type each line twice:

One space
before and
after the sign
&. Type
policy
numbers,
order
numbers,
invoice
numbers,
without
commas.

```
& & & j&j j&j j&j Sax & Co., Vim & Zale, Mac & Co.
j&j j&j j&j Call Fox & Co., Gay & Co., Poe & Bond.
Ship at once Webb & Zorn's Order #350 for $492.68.
Mail invoices to Lux & Son, Quin & Co., Tyle & Co.
Joe's Policy #293648 was issued by Wexler & Smith.
```

3. **Balance Sheet with Tabs:**

A balance sheet shows the assets, liabilities, and equity in a business, and hopefully they balance. This is a good practice exercise.

A. Type the following exactly as it appears.

B. Use either the "Tab" key or table feature for the columns.

C. Center the top two lines.

D. Use the underlining feature and boldface.

BALANCE SHEET

For Month Ended June 30

Assets

Cash in Bank	$8,563.75
Accounts Receivable	5,109.25
Notes Receivable	4,060.00
Equipment	25,620.00
Inventory	10,500.00
Total Assets	**$53,853.00**

Liabilities

Accounts Payable	$6,678.00
Notes Payable	4,990.00
Total Liabilities	10,668.00

Owner's Equity

Beginning Investment	$25,523.00
Profit, June 30	20,162.75
Owner's Withdrawals	2,500.75
Owner's Investment	43,185.00
Total Liabilities & Owner's Equity	**$53,853.00**

4. **Paragraph Practice:** Double Spacing.
   Try for a PERFECT copy of each paragraph:

The symbol # typed before a figure stands for   10

the word number. When it is typed after a figure,   20

it stands for the word pounds. This symbol may be   30

used in technical work and in preparing invoices.   40

    1   2   3   4   5   6   7   8   9   10

The symbol & is used only when it is part of   10

the name of a firm. It is correct to write A & P   20

or Simon & Schuster because these firms spell their 30

names this way. But to write Joel & Maxie is poor   40

style unless the reference is to such a firm name.   50

    1   2   3   4   5   6   7   8   9   10

5. **Test Your Skill:** Take Three 3-Minute Timings.

   GOAL: 20 words a minute within 4 errors.
          Record your best speed within 4 errors.

Use double
spacing.

You may have heard it said that Rome was not   10

built in a day. This means, of course, that time   20

and good effort are needed to turn out good work.   30

The idea holds true with your aim to reach a   40

high skill in what you type. To reach this level   50

takes time and good effort. It's the surest way.   60

    1   2   3   4   5   6   7   8   9   10

2. **Letter with Tables:**
   Tables can be used in the body of any document to make key information jump out.

   A. Type the following letter exactly as it appears.

   B. Use either the "Tab" key or table feature for the columns.

April 8,_____

Mr. and Mrs. George N. Cleo
15 Bengal Lane
Albuquerque, NM 87105

Dear Mr. and Mrs. Cleo:

We are pleased to let you know that the following partial order
will be shipped on May 1, _____. Style 443 is on back order and
should be shipped on June 15.

Style 124	1,445 yards
Style 345	2,445 yards
Style 566	566 yards

If you have any questions, please call George Blander at extension 22. Thank you for placing your order with us. We look for-
ward to serving you in the future.

Sincerely,

LESSON 19
% (Percent) ( ) (Parentheses)

1. **Review:** Type each line twice. Double space after each 2-line group.

Alphabet: Ray Fan Ted Hig Wes Vic Bob Max Pol Quen Jack Zoel
     #: d3d d3d d#d did Ship 3# of #31 and 73# of #39 now.
     M: may mid mug; mad mat man; mop mob met; mud mum mew
     N: nut nag not; nip nap nub; now nod new; net nab nib
Speedup: You can make good on any job if you have the urge.

Stretch shift-key finger. Keep other fingers in typing position.

          1   2   3   4   5   6   7   8   9   10

2. **New-Key Practice:** % The % is on the **5-key**. *Use F-Finger.*
   (1) Depress right shift key; (2) Reach for the **5-key**; (3) Move fingers back home. Practice these steps until you can do them smoothly—without looking at your fingers. Then type each line twice:

No space between a number and the sign %.

    % % % f%f f%f f%f Pay 5%; Pay 6%; Pay 7%; Pay 10%;
    f%f f%f f%f Tax of 2%, 3%, 4%, 5%, 6%, 7%, 8%, 9%;
    f%f f%f f%f Get 5% or 6% interest on the $75 bond.
    Max got 10%; Vic got 15%; Zoel got 25%; I got 50%.
    Our 5½% rate on the $2,960 note is reduced to 4½%.

Keep elbows close to body.

3. **New-Key Practice: ( ) Left and Right Parentheses**

   A. The left parenthesis is on the **9-key**. Use **L-Finger**. (1) Depress left shift key; (2) Reach for **9-key**; (3) Move finger back home. When you can do these steps without looking at your fingers, type this drill twice:

       191 1(1 191 1(1 191 1(1 191 1(1 191 1(1 191 1(1

   B. The right parenthesis is on the **0-key**. Use **;-Finger**. (1) Depress left shift key; (2) Reach for **0-key**; (3) Move finger back home. When you can do these steps without looking at your fingers, type this drill twice:

       ;0; ;); ;0; ;); ;0; ;); ;0; ;); ;0; ;); ;0; ;);

   C. Now test your control. Type each line twice; keep elbows close to body.

No space between parentheses and text within them.

    (((1(1 1(1 1(1 The (is the shift of the 9-key.
))) ;); ;); ;); The) is the shift of the 0-key.
    One (1); Two (2); Three (3); Seven (7); Eight (8);
    The reference (the one on page 94) must be quoted.
    July 4 is America's Independence Day (since 1776).

LESSON 29
FORM LETTER, LETTER WITH TABLES,
BALANCE SHEET WITH TABS

Push the envelope! That's a commonly used business expression for taking something as far as you can. Let's take what you've learned so far and push the envelope.

1. **Form Letter:**
   A form letter is one that can be sent to many different people. Most of the letter will remain constant; however, certain parts will change for each recipient. Variable information can include the name, inside address, salutation, dollar amount, dates, locations, or any other information that will differ from one recipient to the next.

   A. Type the following form letter, and put the variable information in parentheses.
   B. Save it. (Refer to your user's manual for instructions on saving a document.)
   C. Call up the document and add the variable information.

```
(Date)

(Name)
(Inside Address)



Dear (name)

Today we received your check in the amount of $ (amount) for the
ABS Foundation. This will help us meet our annual goal of $50,000.
So far we have received $42,000 in pledges.

Thank you for your generous contribution and for helping to reach
our ambitious goal.


Sincerely,
```

---

4. **Paragraph Practice:** Double Spacing.
   Try for a PERFECT copy of each paragraph:

WORDS

All the
numbers
plus the
new keys.

Did you know that in 1965 American women held   10

70% of all national wealth, 80% of all life insur-   20

ance benefits, 65% of all savings accounts, 48% of   30

all railroad stock, and about 23% of all the jobs?   40

    1   2   3   4   5   6   7   8   9   10

Independence Day in the United States is July   10

4 (since 1776). July 4 is Independence Day too in   20

the Philippines (since 1946), and Venezuela (since   30

1821). In Argentina it is on July 9 (since 1810).   40

    1   2   3   4   5   6   7   8   9   10

5. **Test Your Skill:** Take Three 3-Minute Timings.

   GOAL: 20 words a minute within 4 errors.
          Record your best speed within 4 errors.

WORDS

Use
double
spacing.

All typing beginners make errors. You are no   10

exception. So do not get the feeling that you are   20

clumsy with your hands any time you strike one key   30

for another. Just shrug off those errors you make   40

and keep going. Typing is a skill that takes much   50

practice to learn. You and your friends can learn   60

to type by touch. One only needs a zest to learn.   70

    1   2   3   4   5   6   7   8   9   10

Lesson 19: % (Percent) ( ) (Parentheses)   45

1. **Memorandum-Skill Test:** Here are two memoranda. See whether you can arrange them attractively using any of the headings shown.

Memorandum 1

To: All Accounting Personnel/ From: Ethel Maxwell, Supervisor/ Date: *Today's*/ Subject: Computation of Commissions / I would like all of you to please compute the new commissions for our sales personnel inasmuch as the fiscal year will be drawing to a close.

This is to receive priority attention./ *Your initials*

Memorandum 2

To: All Sales Representatives / From: David Dworkin, President / Date: *Today's* / Subject: Sporting Event Tickets

For many years we have been distributing tickets to major sporting events as a Public Relations gesture to many of our leading clients.

Do you feel the business this is generating warrants the expense?

xx

LESSON 20
″ (Quotation Mark)
__ (Underscore)

1. **Review:** Type each line twice. Double space after each 2-line group.

Alphabet: `frfvb jujmn ftfg jyjh dedc kik, swsx lol. aqaz ;p/`
&: `& & j&j j&j Levy & Co., Dix & Son., Smith & Marlon`
%: `f5f f5f f%f f%f I got 15%; Sam, 25%; and Cal, 60%.`
O: `old out ode; one owe oak; owl off oil; ohm oaf ore`
P: `pit pat put; pun pew pen; pad pub pot; paw pay pig`
Speedup: `The old man said the work is too hard for one man.`
         `   1     2     3     4     5     6     7     8     9     10`

2. **New-Key Practice:** ″ **(Quotation Mark)**

   A. The ″ is on the '-key. Use the left shift key and the **;**-finger. Practice the reach: (1) Depress the left shift key; (2) Reach for the apostrophe-key; (3) Move fingers back home. When you can do it smoothly without looking at your fingers, type this drill twice:

   `″ ″ ″ ;″; ;″; ;″; Walt said, "Pat can draw a map."`

   B. Type each line twice, double spacing after each 2-line group.

Use quotation marks to indicate: quoted material; some titles; seconds; and inches. An apostrophe shows possession and is used to denote minutes and feet.

`"Well," Ben asked, "will you introduce me to her?"`
`The teacher said, "Sit erect—as tall as you can."`
`Cal said he likes the rhythm in Poe's "The Raven."`
`Jim Ryun from Kansas ran an indoor mile in 3' 57".`
`The pugilist was knocked out in 2' 10" of Round 8.`

No space between quotation marks and material quoted.

3. **New-Key Practice:** __ **(Underscore)**

The __ is on the hyphen-key. Use **;**-finger. (1) Depress left shift key; (2) Reach for the hyphen-key; (3) Move fingers back home. Practice these steps until you can do them smoothly without looking at your fingers. Then type this drill twice:

`__ __ __ /__/ /__/ The file is called "tenth_edition.doc."`

NOTE: The underscore symbol is useful for creating file names and in typing e-mail addresses. (Example: paul_marx@aol.com.) Words can be underscored by using the font menu, an underscore button, or a keyboard command. Refer to your user's manual.

MEMORANDA

The prime objective of the memorandum is to send ideas, decisions, and suggestions to other members of your organization. The memorandum can be sent on a half or full sheet of paper, depending on the length of the message. If your organization uses memoranda frequently, there will probably be a printed letterhead for memoranda.

1. The body of the memorandum starts three lines from the letterhead. If there is no printed letterhead, type the word MEMORANDUM across the center top portion of the paper.

2. Any of the following headings may be used:

To:	TO:	TO:
From:	FROM:	FROM:
Date:	DATE:	DATE:
Subject:	SUBJECT:	SUBJECT:

3. The left margin should align with the text portion of the heading, and the right margin should equal that of the left.

4. The paragraphs should be single spaced, with double spacing between the paragraphs.

```
                    M E M O R A N D U M


        TO:   The Executive Board

      FROM:   Thomas N. Sherrill, President

      DATE:   September 22, _____

   SUBJECT:   New Insurance Program


            Please be advised that there will be a brief
            meeting on Friday, September 29 at 3p.m. to
            discuss a proposed insurance program.

            All are expected to attend.

            sll
```

4. **Paragraph Practice:** Double Spacing.
   Try for 2 PERFECT copies of this paragraph:

Use
double
spacing.

```
    The Americans characterize speech that is not        10

entirely clear by saying "That's Greek to me"; the       20

Russians and Roumanians by "That's Chinese to me";       30

the French by "That's Hebrew to me"; and the Poles       40

by "That's Turkish to me." All have the same idea.       50

      1     2     3     4     5     6     7     8     9    10
```

5. **Test Your Skill:** Take Three 3-Minute Timings.

   GOAL: 20 words a minute within 4 errors.
          Record your best speed within 4 errors.

WORDS

Use
double
spacing.

```
    Courage is the nerve to last a trifle longer.        10

John quit his job and applied for a new one there.       20

Fortune smiles on the few--and laughs at the many.       30

A grudge is too heavy a load for anybody to carry.       40

To be calm under stress is the true sign of power.       50

Things will come your way--when you go after them.       60

Ideas must work or they are no better than dreams.       70

      1     2     3     4     5     6     7     8     9    10
```

Address on Letter and Envelope	Salutation and Complimentary Close
(20) *Professor at a College or University* Professor (full name) Name of Institution City, State, Zip Code	Dear Professor (last name): Sincerely yours,
(21) *Protestant Clergyman* Reverend (full name) Street City, State, Zip Code	Dear Reverend (last name): Sincerely yours,
(22) *Roman Catholic Priest* Reverend (full name) Street City, State, Zip Code	Dear Reverend Father: Sincerely yours,
(23) *Rabbi* Rabbi (full name) Street City, State, Zip Code	Dear Rabbi: Sincerely yours,
(24) *General, U. S. Army* General (full name) Address of Station	Dear General (last name): Sincerely yours,
(25) *Captain, U. S. Navy* Captain (full name) Address of Station	Dear Captain (last name): Sincerely yours,

LESSON 21
@ (At) * (Asterisk)

1. **Review:** Type each line twice. Double space after each 2-line group.

Alphabet: `Jacquel W. Parky did give them five boxes of zinc.`
( ): `191 1(1 ;0; ;); (one) (two) (three) (four) (seven)`
": `" " " s "s s"s s"s Gwen said, "Show me how to sew."`
Q: `aqua quay quit quip; quiz quest; quiet quail quart`
R: `raw rap rut; rug rub rob; rid run rip; red ray row`
Speedup: `Last year all the work was done just at this time.`

`    1    2    3    4    5    6    7    8    9    10`

Reach for all top-row keys without looking up.

2. **New-Key Practice: @ (At)**

One space before and after the sign @.

A. @ is on the **2**-key. Use right shift key and **S**-finger. Practice the reach: (1) Depress right shift key; (2) Reach for the **2**-key; (3) Move fingers back home. When you can do these steps without looking at your fingers, type this drill twice:

`@ @ @ s@s s@s s@s Get 90 @ $2; 62 @ $20; 72 @ $21.`

B. Type each line twice:

`The symbol @ means at or per; as 150 dozen @ $9.70.`
`Ship 12 gross (1928) @ $80.65 (less 10% discount).`
`Buy 10 @ $56; 125 @ $28; 374 @ $39; and 905 @ $68.`
`Send us 12 boxes @ $59 and another 12 boxes @ $60.`
`Try to ship 10 @ $16, 28 @ $47, and 30 @ $59 each.`

3. **New-Key Practice: * (Asterisk)**

The asterisk may be put before or after a word.

A. The * is on the **8**-key. Use **K**-finger. (1) Depress left shift key; (2) Reach for **8**-key; (3) Move fingers back home. Practice these steps until you can do them smoothly without looking at your fingers. Then type this drill twice:

`* * * k*k k*k k*k Use the asterisk* for footnotes.`

B. Type each line twice. Double space after each 2-line group.

All the alphabet keys.

`This symbol * (asterisk) is the shift of the 8-key.`
`Special items are marked with the *; as, 50*, 68*.`
`The * directs you to extra text at bottom of page.`
`Jackie used the symbol * quite often in her essay.`
`When Prof. Broz* arrived, I requested him to wait.`

Address on Letter and Envelope	Salutation and Complimentary Close
(10) *Librarian of Congress* Honorable (full name) Librarian of Congress Washington, D. C. 20540	```Dear Mr./Ms. (last name):``` ```Sincerely yours,```
(11) *Comptroller General* Honorable (full name) The Comptroller General of the United States Washington, D. C. 20548	```Dear Mr./Ms. (last name):``` ```Sincerely yours,```
(12) *The Chief of Justice* The Chief Justice The Supreme Court Washington, D. C. 20543	```Dear Mr./Madam Chief Justice:``` ```Sincerely yours,```
(13) *Associate Justice* Mr./Ms. Justice (last name) The Supreme Court Washington, D. C. 20543	```Dear Mr./Ms. Justice:``` ```Sincerely yours,```
(14) *Judge of a Court* Honorable (full name) Judge of the (name of court) Street City, State, Zip Code	```Dear Judge (last name):``` ```Sincerely yours,```
(15) *Clerk of a Court* Mr./Ms. (full name) Clerk of the (name of court) Street City, State, Zip Code	```Dear Mr./Ms. (last name):``` ```Sincerely yours,```
(16) *Governor of a State* Honorable (full name) Governor of (State) City, State, Zip Code	```Dear Governor (last name):``` ```Sincerely yours,```
(17) *Secretary of State (of a State)* Honorable (full name) Secretary of State of (State) City, State, Zip Code	```Dear Mr./Ms. Secretary:``` ```Sincerely yours,```
(18) *Mayor* Honorable (full name) Mayor of (City) City, State, Zip Code	```Dear Mayor (last name):``` ```Sincerely yours,```
(19) *President of a College or University* President (full name) Name of Institution City, State, Zip Code	```Dear President (last name):``` ```Sincerely yours,```

4. **Paragraph Practice:** Double Spacing.
   Try for a PERFECT copy of each paragraph:

Use double
spacing.

```
    A Roman story tells of a tutor and his pupil,       10

a very young Prince. The lesson was in Roman His-        20

tory and the Prince was unprepared. "Now, we come       30

to the Emperor Caligula*," said the tutor. "Do you      40

know anything about him, Prince?" He didn't know.       50

        1     2     3     4     5     6     7     8     9    10
```

```
    The tutor's question brought no response from        10

the Prince. The silence was getting embarrassing,       20

when it was broken by the tactful tutor, who said:      30

"Your Highness is right--perfectly right. For the       40

less said about the Emperor Caligula, the better."      50

        1     2     3     4     5     6     7     8     9    10
```

```
* A very cruel Roman Emperor born A.D. 12, and assassinated by
  conspirators A.D. 41.
```

5. **Test Your Skill:** Take Three 2-Minute Timings.

   GOAL: 20 words a minute within 4 errors.
          Record your best speed within 4 errors.

WORDS

All the
alphabet
keys.

```
    No type of job you have is worthwhile if you        10

do the work lazily till quitting time. If you are       20

eager to make good in business or any other field,      30

get into the type of work in which you can put in       40

full time and exert your best efforts for success.      50

        1     2     3     4     5     6     7     8     9    10
```

SPECIAL FORMS OF ADDRESS, SALUTATION, AND COMPLIMENTARY CLOSE

Special forms of address, salutation, and complimentary close are used for people in high official positions and in special professions. The following forms are commonly used in addressing government officials, educators, clergy, and members of the armed forces:

Address on Letter and Envelope	Salutation and Complimentary Close
(1) *The President* The President The White House Washington, D. C. 20500	Dear Mr./Ms. President: Respectfully yours,
(2) *The Vice President* The Vice President United States Senate Washington, D. C. 20510	Dear Mr./Ms. Vice President: Sincerely yours,
(3) *Member of Cabinet* The Honorable (full name) The Secretary of (Dept.) Washington, D. C. 20511	Dear Mr./Madam Secretary: Sincerely yours,
(4) *Postmaster General* The Honorable (full name) The Postmaster General Washington, D. C. 20260	Dear Mr./Ms. Postmaster General: Sincerely yours,
(5) *The Attorney General* The Honorable (full name) The Attorney General Washington, D. C. 20530	Dear Mr./Ms. Attorney General: Sincerely yours,
(6) *American Ambassador* The Honorable (full name) American Ambassador City, Country	Dear Mr./Madam Ambassador: Very truly yours,
(7) *United States Senator* Honorable (full name) United States Senate Washington, D. C. 20510	Dear Senator (last name): Sincerely yours,
(8) *Speaker of the House of Representatives* Honorable (full name) Speaker of the House of Representatives Washington, D. C. 20510	Dear Mr./Ms. Speaker: Sincerely yours,
(9) *Representative* Honorable (full name) House of Representatives Washington, D. C. 20515	Dear Mr./Ms. (last name): Sincerely yours,

6. **Test Your Skill:** Take Three 4-Minute Timings.
   Follow these steps in all your 4-minute timings.

   A.   Repeat if you finish before end of 4 minutes.
   B.   After each timing, jot down total words typed and total errors.
        Practice the words that have errors till they are easy for you.
   C.   Your 4-minute speed is words typed divided by 4.
   D.   Record on your Progress Chart (page 136) your best speed within 4 errors.

   GOAL: 22 words a minute within 4 errors.
           Double spacing.

	WORDS
Some people do not practice what they preach;	10
they just do not have more time left for practice.	20
Thrift is doing without something you want so	30
that one day you can buy something you don't need.	40
It's no wonder that King Solomon was so wise:	50
he had 500 wives whom he consulted when uncertain.	60
Doctors tell us that exercise is good for us;	70
so why does it make us feel so tired when we stop?	80
Science can now pinpoint all of our problems;	90
but the only trouble is that it cannot solve them.	100

           1   2   3   4   5   6   7   8   9   10

FOLDING AND INSERTING A LETTER

For a Small Envelope: *3 Folds*

1. Bring the bottom edge up to about ¼ inch from the top edge and crease.

2. Bring the right edge toward the left about ⅓ the width of the paper and crease.

3. Bring the left edge almost to the last fold and crease.

4. Insert the folded letter:

    (a) Hold the envelope with reverse side facing you.

    (b) Insert the letter, last crease first.

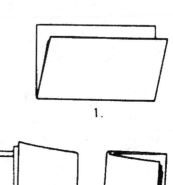

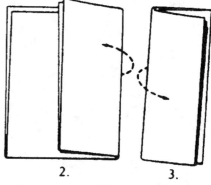

For a Large Envelope: *2 Folds*

1. Bring bottom edge up to ⅓ the length of the paper and crease.

2. Bring top edge down to almost the first crease, leaving a margin of about ¼ inch, and crease.

3. Insert the folded letter:

    (a) Hold the envelope with reverse side facing you.

    (b) Insert the letter, last crease first.

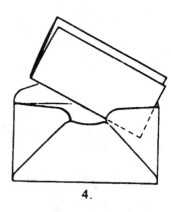

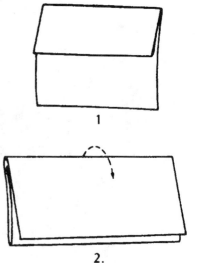

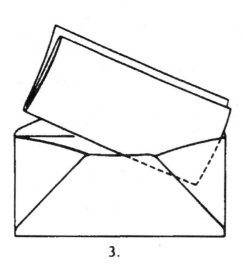

LESSON 22
HORIZONTAL AND VERTICAL ALIGNMENT

1. **Review:** Type each line twice. Double space after each 2-line group.

Alphabet:	The broken trapeze was quickly fixed by Jim Gavor.
S:	sap sun sit; sir sob sol; sub six sew; say sod sip
T:	top tap tug; tip tan toe; tag ten try; tar tow tub
Underscore:	j__j j__j j__j We must wear a tuxedo at the ceremony.
	;__; ;__; ;__; I must submit my book report tomorrow.
Speedup:	To get more pay for the work, you must do it well.

Keep hands and arms still; let the fingers do the work.

```
          1    2    3    4    5    6    7    8    9    10
```

2. There are four ways to align text horizontally. Refer to your user's manual.

Left Align:

```
Everything will be to the left. This was the only style with a
typewriter, and is still very popular with computers.
```

Center:

```
    Everything will be centered. With a typewriter this was done
manually; now it's a snap. This is popular for headings, invita-
                    tions, and announcements.
```

Right Align:

```
          Everything will be to the right. This is also popular for
                    headings, invitations, and announcements.
```

Full Justify:

```
Left and right margins will be flush. This was used extensively when
computers first hit the scene. Be careful! This can cause weird
spacing. Your text might look as if rivers are running down the
page.
```

State Abbreviations

(All Capitals—Without Period)

Alabama	**AL**	Illinois	**IL**	Montana	**MT**	Puerto Rico	**PR**
Alaska	**AK**	Indiana	**IN**	Nebraska	**NB**	Rhode Island	**RI**
Arizona	**AZ**	Iowa	**IA**	Nevada	**NV**	South Carolina	**SC**
Arkansas	**AR**	Kansas	**KS**	New Hampshire	**NH**	South Dakota	**SD**
California	**CA**	Kentucky	**KY**	New Jersey	**NJ**	Tennessee	**TN**
Colorado	**CO**	Louisiana	**LA**	New Mexico	**NM**	Texas	**TX**
Connecticut	**CT**	Maine	**ME**	New York	**NY**	Utah	**UT**
Delaware	**DE**	Maryland	**MD**	North Carolina	**NC**	Vermont	**VT**
D. C.	**DC**	Massachusetts	**MA**	North Dakota	**ND**	Virginia	**VA**
Florida	**FL**	Michigan	**MI**	Ohio	**OH**	Washington	**WA**
Georgia	**GA**	Minnesota	**MN**	Oklahoma	**OK**	West Virginia	**WV**
Hawaii	**HI**	Mississippi	**MS**	Pennsylvania	**PA**	Wisconsin	**WI**
Idaho	**ID**	Missouri	**MO**	Oregon	**OR**	Wyoming	**WY**

Practice in Addressing Envelopes

To each address below, type a small envelope; then a large envelope. First: Review the directions on page 79.

```
Jason & Company, Inc. / 472 Elem Avenue / Philadelphia, PA 25409 /
    (HOLD)
Fenton Tool Works, Inc. / 310 Court Street / Dallas, TX 43621
White Repair Shop, Inc. / Attention: Mr. Sam Paley / 197 Beacon
    Street / Newark, NJ 31829
```

Use all
caps
method.

```
Minton Brothers, Inc. / 385 Oakley Building / Yonkers, NY 27065 /
    (SPECIAL DELIVERY)

Acme Film Company / 641 Broadway / Providence, RI 84062
Dr. George Kane / 615 Morton Lane / Portland, OR 75910 / (PERSONAL)
```

Addressing Very Large Envelopes

To address a very large envelope (Manilla, bubble bag, etc.):

1. Type the address on a label.

2. Paste the label in about the center of the envelope.

   Note: Envelopes can be generated from the envelopes & labels option from the tools menu. Refer to your user's manual.

Following is the top portion of the screen on Microsoft Word showing the alignment buttons on the toolbar.

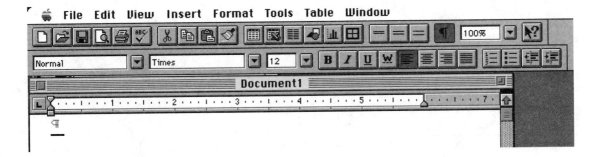

3. **Practice Horizontal Alignment:** Type the following paragraph.

   In Kansas, there's a law that reads: "When two trains approach each other at a railroad crossing, both shall come to a full stop and neither shall start up again until the other has gone."

   A. Left Align the above text.
   B. Center the above text.
   C. Right Align the above text.
   D. Full Justify the above text.

4. **Practice Vertical Alignment:** Type the following text.

   WHAT'S A MODEM?

   A modem is a device that gives you the ability to communicate with other computers. It connects the computer with the ordinary telephone lines, which carry information in the form of electronic impulses to or from users at other locations.

   A. Center the title.
   B. Look in the page preview to see how the text is aligned vertically.
   C. Return to the normal view and space down using the "Enter" key until the text is in the center of the page.
   D. Look at the page preview again and repeat until the text is vertically centered on the page.

5. **Paragraph Practice:** Double Spacing.

   A. Type each paragraph twice—slowly, smoothly.
   B. Practice each word that has an error.
   C. Try for a PERFECT copy of each paragraph.

ADDRESSING ENVELOPES

```
DAVID GOODRICH
1258 REED AVE
SCRANTON PA 24917
```

```
CLARK & RICHARDS INC
ATTENTION LEGAL DEPT
378 COURT ST
MACON GA 41302
```

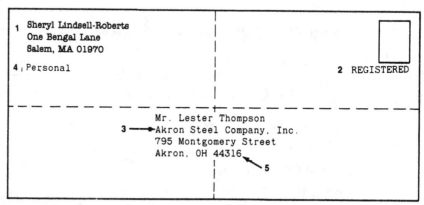

Standard small envelope is 6½ × 3⅝ inches.
Standard large envelope is 9½ × 4⅛ inches.

NOTE: The address typed in all capital letters—without punctuation—conforms to the recommendations of the U.S. Postal Service. (Observe the abbreviations of AVE, ST, BLVD, RD, etc.)

The numbers in the figures are explained below. (The broken lines show the vertical and horizontal centers.)

1.	Return Address: (If not printed)	Block form, single space. Begin on line 3 from top edge and 3 spaces from left edge.
2.	Postal Notation:	Type under the stamp any special postal notations such as REGISTERED, SPECIAL DELIVERY, CERTIFIED, etc.
3.	Mailing Address:	Block form, single space. Type the name at the estimated vertical center. This would be on line 12 of a small envelope, line 14 of a large envelope, line 10 of a postal card. Start it about ½ inch to the left of the center point.
4.	Special In-House Notations:	Type special notations for the company such as Attention, Personal, Please Forward, Hold, etc. under the return address.
5.	Zip Code:	Type the Zip Code 1 space after the state. Use the 2-letter state abbreviations listed on page 80, approved by the U.S. Postal Service.

All the
number
keys.

	WORDS
Christopher Sholes, born on February 14, 1819,	10
made the first practical typewriter. In 1868, he	20
obtained a patent for it. Touch typing, though,	30
was first introduced in 1878 by Frank E. McGurrin.	40

    1   2   3   4   5   6   7   8   9   10

Oliver Wendell Holmes was born March 8, 1841.	10
He graduated from Harvard in 1861 and from Harvard	20
Law School in 1866. He was appointed a Justice of	30
the Supreme Court in 1902. He died March 6, 1935.	40

    1   2   3   4   5   6   7   8   9   10

6. **Test Your Skill:** Take Three 2-Minute Timings.

> GOAL: 18 words a minute within 4 errors.
>   Record your best speed within 4 errors.

Use double
spacing.

	WORDS
Good skill, of course, will help you get that	10
job. Yet it is not enough to make you hold it and	20
get ahead in it. You must also learn to work well	30
with the others in a helpful and energetic spirit.	40

    1   2   3   4   5   6   7   8   9   10

TWO-PAGE LETTERS

Most business letters require only one page. If a letter is too long for one page:

1. End the page with a complete paragraph if you can; if you cannot, leave at least 2 lines and carry over at least 2 lines to page 2.

2. On page 2, type the addressee's name, the page number, and the date. These may be blocked at the left margin or spread evenly across the page. See models below.

3. Continue the letter 3 lines below the page 2 heading.

4. When printing, use plain paper (without letterhead) of the same size and quality as page 1.

Always used for full block.

```
Times Appliance Company, Inc.
Page 2
April 12, _____


Your instructions will be followed exactly. Detailed prices and a
total for each part are listed. We shall
```

Used for all other styles.

```
Mr. Charles H. Andrews      2      June 6, _____


If the plans are changed, we shall submit a revised list to you.
If the plans are not changed, we are ready
```

LESSON 23
TABULATING

1. **Tab Stops:**
   Tabs are used to indent paragraphs, create table columns, or indent other types of text. Most word processing programs have preset tab stops every half inch across the top scale. Using these preset tabs will give you fast document preparation and efficiency. Refer to your user's manual for instructions on changing the tab stops and alignments and adding leaders.

2. **Checking Preset Tab Stops:**

   A. Start at the margin.
   B. Press the [Tab] key until you have run it across the page.

3. **Practice Using the Preset Tab:**

   A. Type the following paragraph.
   B. Press the [Tab] key once to indent the first line.

   "Word processing" is a relatively new term with a very old history. As far back as one can recall, man has been seeking the most efficient ways to process information. When early cavemen inscribed their drawings on the walls of caves, they were processing words. When our founding fathers wrote the Declaration of Independence with their quill pens, they were processing words.

4. **Practice Using the Preset Tab for Two Columns:**

   A. Type the following two columns.
   B. Press the [Tab] key two times to start the first column.
   C. Press the [Tab] key two times between each column.

Marc Lindsell	Architect
Eric Lindsell	Chiropractor

2. **Letter-Skill Test:** Here are two average-length, unarranged letters. See whether you can arrange them attractively in any style. Use today's date.

Letter 1

Mr. John Clarkson, Manager/ Boyntex Auto Supplies, Inc./ 240 Madison Boulevard/ Milwaukee, WI 18107 Dear Mr. Clarkson: Within the next few months you may expect to receive requests for information concerning the new tubeless tires that have recently been developed. There will no doubt be a great demand for these tires because their many unusual features afford maximum riding comfort and ease of driving.

We plan to include in our stock a complete line of this superior product. There may be some delay, however, as manufacturers are having difficulty meeting the current demand.

Don't forget to include your initials. A small shipment that may be used for display purposes should reach you this week. Please inform your customers that we shall do our best to fill their orders promptly./ Sincerely yours,/ HARMON TIRE COMPANY, INC./ George Rice/ Sales Manager

(106 Words)

Letter 2

Mr. William T. Ford/ Federal Insurance Company/ 283 Doyle Drive, Bangor, ME 04401 Dear Mr. Ford: We are very sorry to learn that the public address system we installed two months ago has not been working satisfactorily. We assure you that we will correct this situation at once.

You realize that it is difficult for us to tell you the exact reason for its failure until we make a complete inspection. However, it is quite possible that some of the tubes are defective or that one of the loudspeakers is not in perfect condition.

As you suggested, one of our engineers will phone you next week for an appointment to visit you. At that time, he will make all necessary repairs. Yours truly,/ PUBLIC ADDRESS SYSTEMS, INC./ Henry J. Silver/ Chief Inspector

(105 Words)

5. **Practice Using the Preset Tab for Three Columns:**

  A. Type the following three columns.

  B. Press the [Tab] key two times to start the first column.

  C. Press the [Tab] key two times between each column.

  D. Underline the column headings.

<u>Salespeople</u>	<u>Sales</u>	<u>Commissions</u>
Barbara Lekander	$5,000	$500
Robert Littlehale	$7,470	$747
Beth Wolf	$8,600	$860
Donna Randall	$9,760	$976

  NOTE: In the next chapter you will learn to use the tables and columns feature, which can substitute for the tab in some instances.

6. **Paragraph Practice:** Double Spacing.
  Try for a PERFECT copy of each paragraph:

WORDS

All the
number
keys.

Franklin D. Roosevelt, born January 30, 1882,   10

became President March 4, 1933. He was re-elected   20

in 1936, 1940, 1944. On August 14, 1941, he aided   30

in drafting the structure of the Atlantic Charter.   40

   1   2   3   4   5   6   7   8   9   10

After the attack on Pearl Harbor, December 7,   10

1941, he began to plan for victory in World War 2.   20

In Axis aggression he saw a threat to our liberty.   30

He died at Warm Springs, Georgia, April 12, 1945.   40

   1   2   3   4   5   6   7   8   9   10

LESSON 28
ADDITIONAL LETTERS, 2-PAGE LETTERS, ENVELOPES, AND MEMORANDA

1. **Letter Practice:** Copy Model 1 exactly.

   Model 1: Long Business Letter, Full Block Style

<table>
<tr><td>On Line 12</td><td>October 28, ____</td></tr>
<tr><td>Start 4 lines below date.</td><td>Mr. Joseph Wagner
175 Turnpike Road
Boston, MA 02139</td></tr>
</table>

On Line 12

Start 4 lines below date.

October 28, ____

Mr. Joseph Wagner
175 Turnpike Road
Boston, MA 02139

Dear Mr. Wagner:

Do you need extra money again this year?

You know from past experience that if you start selling Christmas Cards early, you make the most money. Your complete set of samples is ready and waiting for you. Again you will have the first opportunity to show your customers the best-designed and most value-packed assortment in the greeting card industry.

Our FABULOUS FOILS Christmas Assortment contains 11 of the most beautiful cards you ever saw, and costs your customer only $10. These same 11 cards, if sold separately, cost up to $1.75 a card in any store. So you give your customer a $19.25 value for only $10.00.

You make $3 for selling 1 box; $6 for selling 2 boxes; $30 for selling 10 boxes; $150 for selling 50 boxes, etc., of our FABU-LOUS FOILS. Everybody buys at least 1 box of Christmas Cards. Many buy 4 and 5 boxes. So you make $3, $6, or even $15 on almost every call.

Your new sample kit contains 4 boxes, all different. You may return them at our expense anytime within 20 days. Just fill in the card enclosed and mail it today.

1 blank line

Sincerely,

FABULOUS FOILS, INC.

Norman S. Kelvin
Sales Manager

HC
Enclosure

(200 Words)

LESSON 24
TABLES AND COLUMNS

1. **Tables:**
   Tables are useful for showing large numbers of specific, related facts or statistics in a small space. Following is the top portion of the screen on Microsoft Word showing the table button. You can also use the "Table" pull down menu.

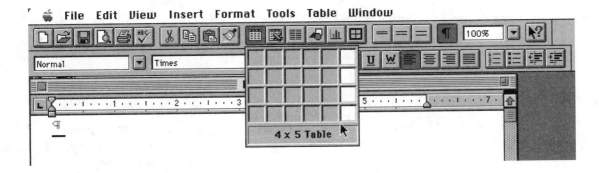

2. **Columns:**
   Columns are useful for newsletters, reports, proposals, manuals, etc. Following is the top portion of the screen on Microsoft Word showing the columns button and pull-down options.

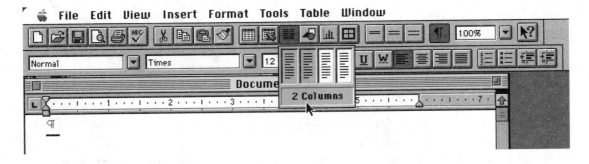

3. **Table Practice:** Table without Rules

   A. Set your computer for 3 columns and 4 rows. Then include the following information. Refer to your user's manual to adjust the width of the columns.

Part Number	Description	Price
123-56	Hose Assembly	$3.50
753-33	Adaptor	$1.10
561-07	Diverter Valve	$9.99

6. **Letter-Skill Test:** Below are two average-length, unarranged letters. See whether you can arrange them attractively. Use today's date.

Letter 1 (Semiblock Style)

Indent all paragraphs 5 spaces.

Mr. James T. Reid/ Acme Realty Company/ 394 Seventh Avenue/ Atlanta, GA 31403/ Dear Mr. Reid: In response to your request, we shall be glad to submit an estimate for installing two elevators in the new apartment house you are building at 286 Park Boulevard. We are happy to have this opportunity to serve you and will mail an itemized bid by the end of next week.

Include your initials. Do not include the "P.S." notation in the letter.

Although our bid may not be the lowest you receive, may we ask that you consider these facts before awarding the contract: We have been in business in this city for over 60 years and manufacture a high-grade product. We enjoy a reputation for excellent workmanship.

If you decide to deal with our concern, we assure you of thorough satisfaction. Yours truly, SWEM & CO., INC. Samuel Hoffman, Chief Engineer/ Furthermore, our one-year guarantee provides complete and regular inspections.

(122 Words)

Letter 2 (Simplified Style)

Bryant Hardware, Inc./ 372 Farragut Street/ Philadelphia, PA 19142/ SUBJECT: LUXOR FANS/ Thank you for your interest in our Luxor Fans. Our representative, Mr. Fred Karlin, has been instructed to call on you within ten days. Mr. Karlin will make a definite appointment by telephone.

Our booklet listed only 60-cycle models because this is the type most commonly ordered. However, we can supply 40-cycle motors in any model without extra charge. Mr. Karlin will discuss this matter with you in detail.

All reports indicate that when hot weather comes there will be a strong demand for the new Luxor Fans with their durable motors and attractive colors. Demand should result in increased profits, and we want you to have your share./ George Flexner, President

(111 Words)

Lesson 27: Business Letters, Semiblock and Simplified Styles

First highlight the table.

B. **Add inside borders** using either the inside border button or the borders option from the format pull down menu.

C. **Add outside borders** using either the outside border button or the borders option from the format pull down menu.

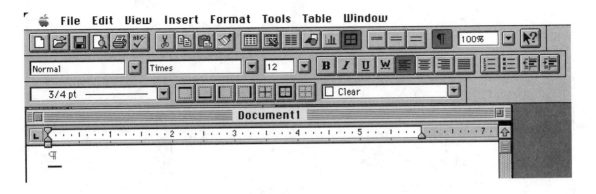

B.

Part Number	Description	Price
123-56	Hose Assembly	$3.50
753-33	Adaptor	$1.10
561-07	Diverter Valve	$9.99

C.

Part Number	Description	Price
123-56	Hose Assembly	$3.50
753-33	Adaptor	$1.10
561-07	Diverter Valve	$9.99

4. **Column Practice:** One column

A. Type the following text.

Perhaps the compulsion to make videos dates back to those Andy Hardy movies. "Hey, kids, let's put on a show in the barn." Once you've had the urge, it's difficult to shake. Conventional wisdom used to rear its ugly head and tell us that videos were too costly. But no longer. With a little ingenuity, a telephone, a VCR, a computer, and a camcorder (and it doesn't have to be yours), you can create videos on a shoestring.

Regardless of the type of video you prepare, whether it's a marketing or sales effort, an orientation program, a training presentation, or a tool for problem solving, you can employ the same tactics.

5. **Letter-Skill Test:** Below is an average-length business letter. Type it 2 times: once in the Semiblock style, like Model 3; and once in the Simplified style, like Model 4.

LETTERHEAD

July 17, _____

Hamilton Bags, Inc.
Attention: Mr. Tom Galati
382 North Avenue
Chicago, IL 60609

Ladies and Gentlemen:

Subject: Order No. 8198

I am very much disappointed with your service in filling my order of July 10 for Blue Patent Leather Handbags.

The package reached me this morning. When I examined the bags, I found that they were not the style I ordered. I specified Model DX, as advertised in THE TRIBUNE, with no initials embossed under the snaplock. You sent Model A, which is entirely too small for my needs, and some contained initials.

I am returning the handbags to you today by insured parcel post and would appreciate it if you would send the correct hand-bags promptly. I am starting my big sale on July 30 and would like to have the handbags by that time.

Thank you for your attention to this matter.

Sincerely yours,

Jane Murphy, Manager

JM/fb

(126 Words)

Lesson 27: Business Letters, Semiblock and Simplified Styles

First highlight the text.

B. Divide the text into two columns using the columns button as shown at the beginning of this chapter.

NOTE: In Normal View, columns will be seen as one long block of text. Choose Page Layout View to see the actual column set-up.

Perhaps the compulsion to make videos dates back to those Andy Hardy movies. "Hey, kids, let's put on a show in the barn." Once you've had the urge, it's difficult to shake. Conventional wisdom used to rear its ugly head and tell us that videos were too costly. But no longer. With a little ingenuity, a telephone, a VCR, a com- puter, and a camcorder (and it doesn't have to be yours), you can create videos on a shoestring.

Regardless of the type of video you prepare, whether it's a marketing or sales effort, an orien- tation program, a training presentation, or a tool for problem solving, you can employ the same tac- tics.

C. Divide the text into three columns using the columns button. (First highlight the text.)

NOTE: In Normal View, columns will be seen as one long block of text. Choose Page Layout View to see the actual column set-up.

Perhaps the com- pulsion to make videos dates back to those Andy Hardy movies. "Hey, kids, let's put on a show in the barn." Once you've had the urge, it's diffi- cult to shake. Conventional wis- dom used to rear its ugly head and tell us that videos were too costly. But no longer. With a little ingenuity, a telephone, a VCR, a computer, and a camcorder (and it doesn't have to be yours), you can create videos on a shoe- string. Regardless of the type of video you prepare, whether it's a marketing or sales effort, an orien- tation program, a training presenta- tion, or a tool for problem solv- ing, you can em- ploy the same tactics.

5. **Test Your Skill:** COBOL Exercise
COBOL is the self-documenting computer language that uses the vocabulary of the business world. It can produce numeric and alphabetic information.

A. Type the following text exactly as you see it.

B. You might use a monospacing font, such as Courier.

4. **Letter Practice:** In the Simplified style, the salutation and complimentary closing are omitted. The subject line appears in all capital letters three lines below the inside address and three lines above the body. The writer's name appears four lines below the body, also in all capital letters. All parts of this letter style are blocked; therefore, no tabs need to be set. Type a copy of Model 4.

Model 4
Short Business Letter
Simplified Style
Single Spaced

```
April 20, _____

Mr. Lester Thompson
Harmon Silk Co., Inc.
376 Montgomery Street
Akron, OH 44316

SUBJECT: BILINGUAL SECRETARIAL POSITION

About two months ago I inquired by letter whether you could use
an experienced bilingual secretary with knowledge of Spanish. You
informed me that you had no openings then but that you would
place my name on file.

Although I am now employed, I am still interested in working for
your Export Division. You will note, by referring to my original
letter of application, that I have all the qualifications for the
job and that I will make an excellent secretary.

May I hear from you soon concerning the prospects of my joining
your export staff.


MEREDITH STONE
```

(100 Words)

```
1       $CONTROL USLINIT,MAP,VERBS
1.1     IDENTIFICATION DIVISION.
1.2     PROGRAM-ID.     RADO95C.
1.3     AUTHOR.         S. SAMPSON.
1.4     INSTALLATION.   GENERAL-CINEMA-BEVERAGES.
1.5     DATE-WRITTEN.   10/30/87.
1.6     DATE-COMPILED.  11/02/87.
1.7
1.8     * [MOD 0 - RADO95C - S. SAMPSON     - 11/02/XX - SR# PRS7504]
1.9     * * * * * * * * * * * * * NEW CODE LOG  * * * * * * * * * * *
2       *   WRITTEN BY  : S. SAMPSON                                 *
2.1     *   DATE WRITTEN: 02 NOVEMBER 19XX                           *
2.2     *   PROGRAM NAME: RADO95C                                    *
2.3     *   SERVICE REQ : PRS7504                                    *
2.4     *    PURPOSE:  TO VERIFY THE PROCESSING DATE ENTERED BY      *
2.5     *              THE USER DURING ROUTE SETTLEMENT BY COMPARING *
2.51    *              IT TO THE DATE IN THE RASYSCNT FILE....       *
2.6     *    PROGRAM LOGIC:                                          *
4.4     *                                                            *
4.5     *    FILES USED: RASTWO4J, RASTWO4S                          *
4.6     * * * * * * * * * * * * * * * * * * * * * * * * * * * * * * *
4.7     * * * * * * * * * PROGRAM MODIFICATION LOG  * * * * * * * * *
4.8     * MOD. MOD.  PROG   S/R              SUMMARY                 *
4.9     *  #   DATE  INIT    #           OF ACTUAL MODIFICATION      *
5       *----------------------------------------------------------*
5.1     *                                                            *
5.2     *----------------------------------------------------------*
5.3     ENVIRONMENT DIVISION.
5.4     CONFIGURATION SECTION.
5.5
5.6     SOURCE-COMPUTER.    HP-3000.
5.7     OBJECT-COMPUTER.    HP-3000.
5.8
5.9     INPUT-OUTPUT SECTION.
6       FILE-CONTROL.
6.1
6.2     SELECT SYSTEM-CONTROL-FILE
6.3         ASSIGN TO "RASYSCNT"
6.4         ORGANIZATION IS SEQUENTIAL
6.5         ACCESS IS SEQUENTIAL
6.6         FILE STATUS IS SYS-CNTRL-STAT.
6.7
6.8     SELECT PROCESS-DATE-FILE
6.9         ASSIGN TO "WORKFILE"
7           ORGANIZATION IS SEQUENTIAL
7.1         ACCESS IS SEQUENTIAL
7.2         FILE STATUS IS PROCESS-DATE-FILE-STAT.
```

3. **Letter Practice:** In the Semiblock style, paragraphs begin one tab stop from the left margin. Type a copy of Model 3.

Model 3
Average-length
Business Letter
Semiblock Style
Mixed Punctuation

December 12, _____

Allen Screvane & Sons
Attention: Eric Laurence
738 Van Alston Avenue
Los Angeles, CA 90017

Ladies and Gentlemen:

   We are enclosing a check for $375 to be credited to our ac-
count. We had expected to pay the full amount when the invoice
became due, and we regret that we are unable to send you a larger
amount at the present time.

   You will recall that the shipment of topcoats did not reach us
until two weeks after the date on which you promised delivery.
This caused a delay in the display of our stock, which resulted
in a slowing up of sales. Collections, too, are still poor in
this town. Accordingly, we shall be unable to pay the balance of
this account before the first of next month.

   We hope you will realize the position we are in and grant us
this extension.

                         Sincerely yours,

                         PERRY BROTHERS, INC.

                         Warren Bergstein
                         Credit Manager

DW
Enclosure

(126 Words)

LESSON 25
PERSONAL LETTERS,
FULL BLOCK AND
MODIFIED BLOCK STYLES

1. **Review:** Type each line twice. Double space after each 2-line group.

Alphabet:	`wavy list neat axle quip from doze high jury backs`
U:	`use unit up bus cub cut; pun put pull; dump dub rub`
V:	`van vow vex vim via vote; vend void vice vase view`
@:	`s@s s@s s@s Ship 12 @ $16; 32 @ $46; and 52 @ $56.`
Speedup:	`The boss may put a new man on this job to help us.`

Try to type without pauses.

```
      1    2    3    4    5    6    7    8    9    10
```

2. **Test Your Skill:** Take Three 4-Minute Timings.

GOAL: 22 words a minute within 4 errors.
Record your best speed within 4 errors.

WORDS

Double
Spacing.

```
   It is now time to use the skills you learned          10

to input a personal letter. This is the kind you         20

send to your family and friends. It is a casual,         30

simple note. You write just as you talk to them.         40

   The parts of the personal letter are: return          50

address, salutation, body, closing, and signature.       60

At all times it is best to use white letter paper.       70

   Be sure you have a neat printout to show you          80

think well of the person to whom you are writing.        90

Study the model on the next page and type a copy.       100
```

```
      1    2    3    4    5    6    7    8    9    10
```

LESSON 27
BUSINESS LETTERS,
SEMIBLOCK AND SIMPLIFIED STYLES

1. **Review:** Type each line twice. Double space after each 2-line group.

```
Alphabet:   Hy Maquel rejected five dozen woody packing boxes.
: (Colon):   : : : ;:; ;:; ;:; Dear Kay: Dear Cora: Dear Wally:
       Y:   you yam yes; yap yew yet; yen yip yak; yea yah yow
       Z:   zero zone zinc; zest zoom zombi; zebra zonal zippy
 Speedup:   Six city boys may come here to get work on a farm.
            1    2    3    4    5    6    7    8    9    10
```

Use a sharp bounce-off tap on the space bar.

2. **Paragraph Practice:** Type the following paragraphs for practice.

```
    You have learned that in the modified block style

business letter all the parts are started from the

left margin, except the date and the closing lines.

You start these lines at the center of your paper.

    The semiblock style letter is almost the

same as the modified block. The only difference is

that here you have to set two tab stops: the first,

five spaces from your left margin to indent every

paragraph; the second, at the center of the paper,

for the date and the closing lines. Take a moment to

study the model on the next page, then type it.
```

3. **Letter Practice:** In the Full Block style, everything starts at the margin.

Model 1
Short Personal Letter
Single Spaced

```
2830 Shore Road
Brooklyn, NY 11220
July 3, _____


Dear Norma,

Would you like to come along with me and mother on an auto trip
to Vermont? We are going to visit my aunt Marilyn. She said she
would be happy to see you.

Aunt Marilyn's house is on a lake, so we'll be able to swim and
canoe, as well as hike in the woods. We plan to leave on Monday,
July 20 and return on Friday, July 24. I hope you can go.

Sincerely,
```

(75 Words)

Letter 3 (Modified Block Style)

Start the date and complimentary closing at the center.

Today's Date / McClure & Rider, Inc./ Attention Thomas N.Sherrill/ 920 Madison Avenue/ New York, NY 10028/ Gentlemen:/ May I ask a favor of you?

As secretary of the Advanced Typing Class at Wadleigh Evening High School, in Manhattan, I am collecting a variety of successful sales letters and circulars for display on our business bulletin board.

Because your agency is so well known for its effective advertising, I would appreciate receiving a few of your mail order samples and circulars.

Thank you for whatever material you can furnish./ Sincerely yours,/ Emma Jones/ *Your initials*

(70 Words)

Letter 4 (Modified Block Style)

Start the date and complimentary closing at the center.

Today's Date / The Personnel Department/ ABC Company, Inc./ 607 Smith Hill Road/ Pasadena, CA 91106/ Dear Mr. Hamill:/ Please consider me a candidate for the Receptionist-Assistant position advertised in THE NEW YORK TIMES on Sunday. I have an excellent administrative background and am skilled at dealing with people.

Although the enclosed resume outlines the details of my background, you will undoubtedly have many questions you would like answered. May I, therefore, have an interview at your convenience?

I would very much like the opportunity to put my skills and talents to work for you./ Very truly yours,/ Janice N. Morton/ *No initials when you sign the letter*

(determine the length)

Lesson 26: Business Letters, Full Block and Modified Block Styles

4. **Letter Practice:** In the Modified Block style, the inside address, date, and complimentary closing start in the center, or slightly to the right of center. Everything else remains as in the Full Block style.

Model 2
Short Personal Letter
Single Spaced

```
                                    275 West Main Street
                                    Newton, NY 12345
                                    April 17, _____

Dear Ralph,

Dr. William Brown, Dean of Admissions at State University, will
speak in the auditorium at Newton High School next Thursday
evening at 7:30. Dr. Brown will talk about the college admission
process, focusing especially on the role parents can play.

I am sure that you would like to hear this talk. Dr. Brown is a
dynamic speaker, and his twenty years of college admission expe-
rience makes him an expert in the field.

The lecture will be followed by a question and answer period. With
your daughter fast-approaching college age, I think you will find
this evening with Dr. Brown both interesting and enlightening.

                                    Sincerely,
```

(103 Words)

5. **Letter-Skill Test:** Following are four short, unarranged letters. See whether you can arrange each on a separate sheet.

Letter 1 (Full Block Style)

Today's Date / The Graphic Magazine/ 725 Clary Street/ Fort Worth, TX 76112/ Ladies and Gentlemen:/ SUBJECT: CONTRACT NO. 762/ Will you please cancel our advertising contract in your publication to take effect immediately.

Business conditions have compelled us to curtail a considerable portion of our advertising appropriation for the next six months.

Much to our regret, we must eliminate the magazine from our list./ Yours truly,/ MARVIN & MAXWELL, INC./ Jack Samuels/ Advertising Manager/ *Your initials*

(45 Words)

Letter 2 (Full Block Style)

Today's Date / Mr. Sidney Harris/ 1756 Leewood Drive/ Hartford, CT 30943/ Dear Mr. Harris:/ Our records show that the bill covering final charges of $27.50 for your gas and electric service has not been paid.

We shall appreciate prompt payment of this bill so that the account may be closed. Payment may be made by mail or in person at any Intercounty Lighting Company office. It is important that you clear up this amount before you move./ Yours sincerely,/ INTERCOUNTY LIGHTING COMPANY/ Vincent Kendall/ Collection Department/ *Your initials*

(63 Words)

5. **Letter-Skill Test:** Below is a short unarranged personal letter. Type it 2 times: once in Full Block style, like Model 1; and once in Modified Block style, like Model 2.

```
Your Home Address
Today's Date

Dear Maxie: Today we learned to type personal letters in the Full
Block and Modified Block styles.

In the Full Block style everything begins at the margin; in the
Modified Block style the inside address, date, and complimentary
closing are centered or slightly to the right of center. Other-
wise, both styles are alike.

Next week we learn to type business letters. As soon as I have
done some of them, I will send you samples.

I am glad to hear that you got the job you were after. Well, I
hope you are happy now and are doing well.

Sincerely,
```

(79 Words)

4. **Letter Practice:** Copy Model 2 *exactly.*

Model 2
Average-length
Business Letter
Modified Block Style
Open Punctuation

August 2, _____

Start on line 15 at center

Start 4 lines below date.

Mrs. Norma Meyers
856 Leonard Street
Newark, NJ 07102

No colon.

Dear Mrs. Meyers

Thank you for your letter of July 27. We are pleased to hear from you and enclose the catalog you desire. It describes in detail the new line of appliances now on display in our local showrooms.

Our stock includes the finest brands with a guarantee for 90 days. For a limited time only, many items are now being offered at greatly reduced prices. There is just a small charge for labor when we make an installation in your home.

If you wish any further details about the equipment we carry, you may call or visit our sales office between the hours of 9 and 5 daily except Sunday. We suggest that you make your choice now in order to benefit from our summer clearance prices.

Cordially yours

DIX APPLIANCE CO., INC.

No comma.

Thomas Benardo
General Manager

RJ
Enclosure

(126 Words)

LESSON 26
BUSINESS LETTERS,
FULL BLOCK AND MODIFIED BLOCK STYLES

1. **Review:** Type each line twice. Double space after each 2-line group.

Depress shift key firmly.

```
Alphabet:  quit wavy exit cubs hems park jolt done zero flags
       W:  wig wax wane; will want wet; wim win won; wit war wish
       X:  box fox nix; fix mix wax; axe fax jax; max hex pox
       *:  k8k k8* k*k k*k The asterisk* is a reference mark.
Speedup:   No man who does not do all the work will get paid.
            1    2    3    4    5    6    7    8    9    10
```

2. **Paragraph Practice:** Type the following paragraph for practice.

Double
Spacing.

```
     A letter that you type to a place of business

is a business letter; it is much like the personal

letter that you practiced in the previous lesson.

In personal letters, your return address, the

date, and the closing lines begin at the top of

the paper and are put in blocked form. But in the

business letter, the return address is on the

letterhead and you have to add the name

and address of the business to which you are

writing. This part is known as the inside address.

Study the model on the next page; then type a copy.
```

3. **Letter Practice:** In the Full Block style, everything begins at the margin.

> **Model 1**
> Short Business Letter
> Full Block Style
> Mixed Punctuation

February 10, _____

Start 4 lines
below date.
Mr. O. V. Poole
409 East 35 Drive
Wichita, KS 67202

Dear Mr. Poole:

SUBJECT: ACCOUNT NO. 8198

Your credit reputation is probably your most valuable asset. Yet you are jeopardizing your credit rating for $79.38, the balance of your account with us.

Since you have ignored our previous four letters, there seems to be no alternative for us except to turn this matter over to our attorneys.

You can make this action unnecessary by mailing your check in the enclosed stamped envelope.

Yours truly,

1 blank line

STAR GOODS CO., INC.

4 blank
lines

John Doe
Vice-President

JN
Enclosure

(67 Words)

SAMPLE BUSINESS LETTER

Sheryl Lindsell-Roberts

(1) Date	September 16, 19—
(2) Mailing/In-House Notation	CERTIFIED MAIL
(3) Inside Address	Jon Allan, Inc.
(4) Attention Line	Attn: Eric Laurence
	24 Parnassus Way
	Tallman, NY 10982
(5) Salutation	Gentlemen:
(6) Subject Line	Subject: Ski Show Contract
(7) Body or Message	I am enclosing the contract we agreed upon stipulating all the terms and conditions of the ski show that will take place at the Marc Alan Community College during the week of December 2.
	Can we meet for lunch on either Wednesday or Thursday of next week in order to finalize arrangements? If neither date is convenient, please call so that we can arrange a mutually convenient time.
(8) Complimentary Closing	Sincerely yours,
(9) Signature Line	Sheryl Lindsell-Roberts
(10) Reference Initials	jt
(11) Enclosure Notation	Enclosure
(12) Copy Notation	pc: Marc Alan Community College
(13) Postscript	The camping show contract will be ready next month.

120 North Street, Marlborough, MA 01752 • (508) 555-1122

Standard Letter Parts

(1) Date Line: Current date with no abbreviations

(2) Mailing Notations: `Special Delivery, Certified Mail, Registered Mail, etc.`

    In-House Notations: `Confidential, Hold, etc.`

(3) Inside Address: Name and address of company or person to whom letter is written

(4) Attention Line: Directly under name of company

(5) Salutation: Must be in accord with first line of inside address ("Ladies and Gentlemen" to a company, "Dear Sir or Madam" to an individual whose name is unknown, or "Dear ——" to an individual whose name is known)

(6) Subject Line: Gives reader theme of letter

(7) Body: Single spaced with double spacing between paragraphs

(8) Complimentary Closing: Only first letter capitalized

Formal	`Yours truly, Very truly yours, Yours very truly, Respectfully, Respectfully yours,`
Informal	`Sincerely, Sincerely yours, Cordially, Cordially yours,`
Personal	`Best wishes, As always, Regards, Kindest regards,`

(9) Signature Line:
```
Very truly yours,          Very truly yours,

                           ABC COMPANY, INC.

John Smith

                           John Smith, President
```

(10) Reference Initials: Initials of typist

(11) Enclosure Notation: When enclosure is being sent with letter (When something is attached, "Attachment" may be used in place)

(12) Copy Notation: When stat copy of letter is being sent to third person ("PC" used for indicating photostatic copy or "BCC" used to send copy when writer does not want to apprise addressee of same. Said notation appears only on the copies—not on the original.)

(13) Postscript: Afterthought or emphasis (do not include "PS" notation)

PLACEMENT OF LETTER

Short Letter   (approximately 125 words or less)
Average Letter (approximately 126–225 words)
Long Letter   (approximately 226 words or more)

NOTE: To see vertical placement, look at the page preview. Refer to your user's manual.

Lesson 26: Business Letters, Full Block and Modified Block Styles